My
Kindle Fire
HDX

Jennifer Kettell

ii

My Kindle Fire HDX

Copyright © 2014 by Pearson Education, Inc.

ISBN-13: 978-0-7897-5293-2
ISBN-10: 0-7897-5293-X

Library of Congress Control Number: 2013957468

Printed in the United States of America

First Printing: February 2014

Trademarks

All terms mentioned in this book that are known to be trademarks or service marks have been appropriately capitalized. Que Publishing cannot attest to the accuracy of this information. Use of a term in this book should not be regarded as affecting the validity of any trademark or service mark.

Warning and Disclaimer

Every effort has been made to make this book as complete and as accurate as possible, but no warranty or fitness is implied. The information provided is on an "as is" basis. The author and the publisher shall have neither liability nor responsibility to any person or entity with respect to any loss or damages arising from the information contained in this book.

Special Sales

For information about buying this title in bulk quantities, or for special sales opportunities (which may include electronic versions; custom cover designs; and content particular to your business, training goals, marketing focus, or branding interests), please contact our corporate sales department at corpsales@pearsoned.com or (800) 382-3419.

For government sales inquiries, please contact governmentsales@pearsoned.com.

For questions about sales outside the U.S., please contact international@pearsoned.com.

Editor-in-Chief
Greg Wiegand

Executive Editor
Loretta Yates

Development Editor
Todd Brakke

Managing Editor
Sandra Schroeder

Project Editor
Mandie Frank

Copy Editor
Barbara Hacha

Indexer
Publishing Works

Proofreader
Dan Knott

Technical Editor
Greg Kettell

Editorial Assistant
Cindy Teeters

Designer
Mark Shirar

Compositor
Tricia Bronkella

Contents at a Glance

Table of Contents

3 Using Amazon's Manage Your Kindle Page 83

About the Author

Jennifer Kettell is the author of *Scrivener Absolute Beginner's Guide* and has written and contributed to dozens of other books about software applications, web design, and digital photography. She also writes fiction. When Jenn isn't writing, she can usually be found curled up with a good book, reading almost a book a day. Jenn has lived all over the United States but currently calls upstate New York home. Visit her website at www.jenniferkettell.com.

Dedication

For my family—Greg Kettell, Roberta Ackerman, Lorraine and Stephen Ravner, Shari and Norman Back, Marcia and Flynn Ravner, and Sharon Ravner, as well as Mandy, Zach, Erica, Jordan, Madison, Reese, Joey, Heather, and Rachael.
And in memory of Dan Ravner.

Acknowledgments

My deepest gratitude and thanks to the many people at Que Publishing who have worked so hard to support me. I'm grateful to Loretta Yates for inviting me to write this book and always brightening a tough day. Huge thanks to Todd Brakke for his editing and sense of humor. Thanks also to Mandie Frank and Barbara Hacha for their production and copyediting expertise. Once again, I appreciate Greg Kettell for reviewing the technical content of this book moments after I finished each chapter—and for always being so supportive of all my writing efforts.

We Want to Hear from You!

As the reader of this book, *you* are our most important critic and commentator. We value your opinion and want to know what we're doing right, what we could do better, what areas you'd like to see us publish in, and any other words of wisdom you're willing to pass our way.

We welcome your comments. You can email or write to let us know what you did or didn't like about this book—as well as what we can do to make our books better.

Please note that we cannot help you with technical problems related to the topic of this book.

When you write, please be sure to include this book's title and author as well as your name and email address. We will carefully review your comments and share them with the author and editors who worked on the book.

Email: feedback@quepublishing.com

Mail: Que Publishing
        ATTN: Reader Feedback
        800 East 96th Street
        Indianapolis, IN 46240 USA

Reader Services

Visit our website and register this book at quepublishing.com/register for convenient access to any updates, downloads, or errata that might be available for this book.

Introduction

You might have purchased your Kindle Fire primarily to read books and watch movies, but the device you hold in your hands can do so much more. After you connect to the Internet and register the Kindle Fire with your Amazon.com account, you'll quickly fill it with books, periodicals, music, videos, apps, and games. You'll use it to browse the Web. You'll even add your own photos and personal documents, making your Kindle Fire uniquely yours.

That's not to say that the Kindle Fire isn't good for reading. You'll have access to millions of books on Amazon.com and other web-sites; many of them are free or cost $2.99 or less. You can borrow books from your local library. When reading is inconvenient, such as when you're driving, you can even have your Kindle Fire read to you, either with an audiobook or using text-to-speech. You're also not limited to books; you can read magazines and newspapers, as well.

The Kindle Fire is primarily intended for consuming content—that is, for reading, listening, or watching. Much of that content is stored in the *cloud*, on Amazon's servers, and you access it over a Wi-Fi or 4G connection. Even if you download content to your device, at which point it becomes device content, a copy stays in the cloud so that it remains accessible from other devices—or if you need to download a new copy. If all that sounds a bit confusing right now, don't worry! Everything will become clear after you read this book.

An Overview of the Various Kindle Fire Models

Other Kindle devices are dedicated e-readers, but the Kindle Fire is also a multimedia entertainment device and a tablet computer. Several models of the Kindle Fire exist, with four models currently supported by Amazon. All of them have access to more than 22 million books, movies, songs, magazines, audiobooks, TV shows, games, and apps. Each model also offers free, unlimited cloud storage for your Amazon content. This book focuses on the Kindle Fire HDX (both the 7- and 8.9-inch models), although many of the tips for using the device apply to the Kindle Fire HD, as well. The processor, display, and storage options vary for each model, as noted here:

- **Kindle Fire HDX:** The new Kindle Fire HDX has a 7-inch screen with 1920×1200 resolution. It contains a Quad-Core 2.2 GHz processor, which makes it three times faster than previous Kindle Fire devices, and offers 11 hours of battery life in mixed use and up to 17 hours of battery life when reading. The HDX has a front-facing HD camera. You can opt for 16, 32, or 64GB of storage and either Wi-Fi only or Wi-Fi plus 4G LTE access (which requires an annual data plan through AT&T or Verizon). Pricing for the Kindle Fire HDX starts at $229 for the 16GB Wi-Fi only and ranges up to $409 for the 64GB Wi-Fi + 4G LTE option.

- **Kindle Fire HDX 8.9":** The Kindle Fire HDX also comes in an 8.9-inch model. This top-of-the-line device contains the same Quad-Core 2.2 GHz processor as the 7-inch HDX, but offers 2560x1600 resolution for crisp, sharp images. The battery life on this model is also better: 12 hours with mixed use and 18 hours while reading. Most important, the HDX 8.9" comes with an 8-megapixel rear-facing camera in addition to its front-facing HD camera. This model is available with 16, 32, or 64GB of storage in either Wi-Fi only or Wi-Fi + 4G LTE versions. The Kindle Fire HDX 8.9" costs $379 for the 16GB Wi-Fi version up to $579 for the 64GB Wi-Fi + 4G LTE option.

- **Kindle Fire HD:** This is essentially the second-generation Kindle Fire (released in 2012) with updates to the operating system and hardware. This device comes with an HD LCD display with 1280×800 resolution. It offers a 1.5GHz dual-core processor, with either 8GB or 16GB of storage. The battery lasts for up to 10 hours of mixed use. This model offers only Wi-Fi and does not have a camera. The Kindle Fire HD costs $139 for the 8GB version and $169 for the 16GB model.

- **Kindle Fire HD 8.9":** Want a larger display on the 2012 model Kindle Fire HD? As its name implies, this model comes with an 8.9-inch HD LCD display with 1920×1200 resolution. The HD 8.9" has a front-facing HD camera and is available with either 16, 32, or 64GB of storage, depending on whether you choose Wi-Fi only or the Wi-Fi + 4G LTE option. Pricing for the Kindle Fire HD 8.9" starts at $229 for the 16GB Wi-Fi version, up to $514 for the 64GB Wi-Fi + 4G LTE device.

Note

Amazon displays what they call "Special Offers" on the lock screens of the device. These ads may offer discounts on items and content purchased on Amazon or contain promotions for movies, music, or video games. You can permanently disable these offers for an additional $15. Personally, I don't find them distracting, because they appear only on the lock screen and not while you are using your device.

What's New on the Kindle Fire

No matter which Kindle Fire model you choose, you will find plenty to do with it. If you're upgrading from a first- or second-generation Kindle Fire, you will be happy to discover many new features. In addition to the upgrades in display, processor, and other hardware enhancements, the new Kindle Fire HDX offers many other improvements.

- Upgraded operating system. The Kindle Fire now runs Fire OS 3.0 "Mojito," a proprietary operating system based on Android.

- Improved color accuracy and brightness for higher-quality video display.

- Improved battery life. When you are reading on your Kindle Fire, the system automatically turns off unused components to extend the battery life even further.

- An 8-megapixel rear-facing camera on the Kindle Fire HDX 8.9" to capture photos of the world around you. Both Kindle Fire HDX models have a front-facing camera to facilitate video chatting.

- Improved position of power and volume control buttons to make it easier to adjust the volume on your device while holding it.

- A "Mayday" button in the Settings screen offering 24/7 live support from Amazon. This feature is available only on the Kindle Fire HDX models.

- Prime Instant Videos available offline. If you have an Amazon Prime membership, you can now download Prime Instant Video movies and TV shows onto your Kindle Fire to view later offline.

- Better content management. The Kindle Fire identifies items that have not been used recently and offers the option of archiving them to the cloud to free up space on your device.

- Better app management. You can switch between multiple apps or content with a side-swipe gesture.

All Kindle Fire models come with a free month of Amazon Prime, if you don't already have an account. Amazon Prime offers unlimited streaming of more than 25,000 movies and TV shows, making it easy to watch a show wherever you have Wi-Fi (or 4G) access. Prime also lets you borrow one free title a month from the Kindle Owners' Lending Library. And if you shop for other products on Amazon.com, you can get free two-day shipping on most items as part of your Prime membership.

What You'll Find in This Book

The Kindle Fire is a tablet computer for people who aren't necessarily computer geeks and who just want to be entertained, read a good book, or have fun—and might have the occasional need to get some work done. *My Kindle Fire HDX* was written with that same mindset. I show you how to get the most fun out of your Kindle Fire HDX and teach you how to access your personal documents when you need to work. However, if you are a computer geek who is new to the Kindle Fire, this book can help you as well.

This book covers all the capabilities of your Kindle Fire. I cover each feature using a step-by-step approach, complete with figures that correspond to each step. You never have to wonder what or where to tap. Each task shows you how to interact with your Kindle Fire using simple symbols that illustrate what you should do.

This icon means that you tap and hold an object on the screen.

This icon means that you drag an item on the screen.

This icon indicates that you pinch on the screen.

This icon means that you spread your thumb and finger on the screen.

This icon indicates that you swipe on the screen.

Along the way, I add plenty of tips that help you better understand a feature or task. If you want to dig deeper, you'll appreciate the Go Further sidebars that provide a more in-depth look at certain features. I also warn you of problems and pitfalls with particular tasks with It's Not All Good sidebars.

How to Navigate This Book

There is a lot to discover about your Kindle Fire. The major functions might be visible to the naked eye, but a lot more hides beneath the surface. As you read this book, you might be surprised to find that your Kindle Fire does more than you ever imagined.

Here are the topics we'll cover in this book.

- Chapter 1, "Getting Started with the Kindle Fire," explains how to set up your device and access the most common settings. You also learn how to operate your Kindle Fire and use the onscreen keyboard. Set up external devices, such as a Bluetooth keyboard, and share your screen with an external display. Finally, learn how to access the new Mayday feature, providing 24/7 personal support for your device.

- Chapter 2, "Accessing Amazon's Cloud Services," covers managing and transferring your content between Amazon's cloud, your personal computer, and your Kindle Fire.

- Chapter 3, "Using Amazon's Manage Your Kindle Page," shows you how to access the Manage Your Kindle page on the Internet, where you can review your Kindle library, rename your Kindle Fire, manage all your Kindle devices and Kindle apps, and much more.

- Chapter 4, "Reading on the Kindle Fire," describes how to find reading material and take advantage of the Kindle Fire's powerful features for reading books, newspapers, magazines, and more.

- Chapter 5, "Listening to Music on the Kindle Fire," shows you how to use your Kindle Fire to play music in your music library (both on your device and in the cloud) and use Amazon's MP3 Store to add to your music collection. You also learn about using playlists and how to view song lyrics.

- Chapter 6, "Watching Video on Your Kindle," covers using your Kindle Fire to stream and download videos from Amazon's video store. You also learn how to convert your own videos to play them on your Kindle Fire. In addition, discover how to use Second Screen to turn your TV into a large display for your movies and use your Kindle Fire as a remote.

- Chapter 7, "Installing and Using Apps," introduces you to the world of apps that dramatically increase the functionality of your Kindle Fire. You learn how to find and install apps, as well as how to deal with misbehaving apps.

- Chapter 8, "Using Social Media and Chat," shows you how to access Facebook and Twitter to stay connected with your friends and how to video chat with them using the Skype app. Discover how to watch YouTube videos on your Kindle Fire. Learn how to connect to Game Circle to challenge your friends and compare scores on your favorite game apps. Finally, learn how to connect with the Goodreads community to read and contribute book reviews.

- Chapter 9, "Reading and Sending Email," shows you how to use your Kindle Fire to read and send email. You also learn how to handle attachments in email.

- Chapter 10, "Managing Your Personal Documents and Data," covers loading, viewing, and editing your personal documents and photos on the Kindle Fire. You also learn how to add and manage contacts and calendars, turning your device into an efficient personal management system.

- Chapter 11, "Taking Photos with Your Kindle Fire HDX," explains how to use the front- and rear-facing cameras on certain models of the Kindle Fire. Discover how to edit those photos and use the filmstrip feature, as well. Finally, learn how to take screenshots from your Kindle Fire.

- Chapter 12, "Browsing the Web with Silk," walks you through using Silk, the web browser that comes with your Kindle Fire. You learn how to access websites, use bookmarks and tabs, and control Silk's behavior.

- Chapter 13, "Giving Your Kids a Kindle Fire," describes how to set up Kindle FreeTime to establish time limits and restrict the content your children can access from their Kindle Fire. I also explain how to sign up for Kindle FreeTime Unlimited, a service that helps take the guesswork out of locating age-appropriate content for your children.

Let's Light This Fire

If you've already gone through the initial setup of your Kindle Fire, you might be tempted to skip ahead to Chapter 2 at this point. I urge you to avoid the rush and at least skim Chapter 1. You won't want to miss some of the new features covered there.

Now that the stage is set, let's light up your Kindle Fire!

View your
Amazon content
from the
Carousel

View content
in each
category

Swipe down
to access
Settings

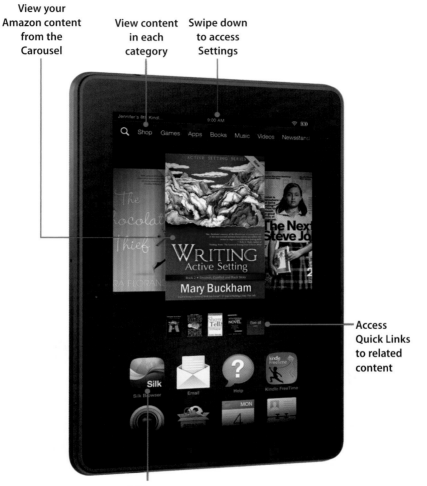

Access
Quick Links
to related
content

Add your
favorite apps
and content to
the home screen

In this chapter, you learn how to connect your Kindle Fire to your Wi-Fi network and register it with Amazon, and you discover the basics of navigating and using your tablet. Topics include the following:

- → The hardware
- → Initial setup
- → The home screen
- → Navigating the Kindle Fire
- → Notifications and options
- → Settings
- → Using the keyboard
- → Connecting to other hardware
- → Searches
- → Help

Getting Started with the Kindle Fire

The Kindle Fire HDX is unassuming at first glance. However, after you power it up, you soon realize that it opens up a new world of entertainment and information. Couple it with Amazon's wide range of services, and the Kindle Fire becomes a truly extraordinary device. In fact, in addition to being a great reading device, your Kindle Fire might replace your computer for some of the things you do on the Internet, especially when you're away from home.

The Kindle Fire is not difficult to use. Many of its features are intuitive, and just by playing with it you can easily discover many of the great tasks it can do. However, if this is your first tablet, you should become familiar with some essentials to get the most from the device. This chapter starts you on the right foot by teaching you about the basic operation of the Kindle Fire.

The Hardware

Your Kindle Fire is equipped with a power button on the back of the device to the left side when in landscape mode (holding the Kindle Fire facing you, with the camera at the top). Press and release this button to power on your Kindle Fire. If the Kindle Fire is already turned on, a quick press of the power button puts it to sleep. Many Kindle Fire covers automatically turn on the device when opened and put it to sleep when closed. Pressing and holding the power button enables you to power off your Kindle Fire.

Should You Power Off?

The display on your Kindle Fire is the primary power consumer on the device. Therefore, your Kindle Fire uses much less power when it's in sleep mode. Obviously, turning it off completely uses even less power, but if you subscribe to a magazine or a newspaper, you won't get your subscription automatically when your Kindle Fire is powered off.

Volume up/down buttons   **Power button**

The volume up/down button is located on the back of the device on the right when the screen is facing you in landscape mode. Press the top half of the button to raise the volume, and press the bottom half to lower it. The dual speakers on the Kindle Fire are at the top of the device, well out of the way of your hands when holding the device in landscape mode. If you want to use headphones or external speakers while listening to music or video, plug them into the 1/4-inch audio plug on the right side of the device, to the right of the volume controls.

On the side of the device, to the left of the power button, is a micro-USB port for charging your Kindle Fire. The Kindle Fire comes with a cable to connect it to a computer so that you can charge the device from your computer's power. You can also use the included wall charger, which charges the Kindle Fire faster and can be used when you're away from your computer.

Initial Setup

When you first turn on your Kindle Fire, you see the lock screen. This screen is usually an ad for a book or other form of Amazon content. Swipe your finger across the lock from right to left to unlock the device. You then go through a series of steps that get you started using your new device. The following three sections take you through each phase of this initial setup.

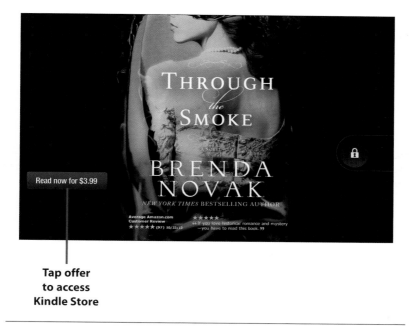

**Tap offer
to access
Kindle Store**

Kindle Fire Updates

It's possible that your Kindle Fire won't have the latest version of the Kindle operating system. If it doesn't, the latest version is downloaded and installed automatically when you set up your Kindle Fire for the first time.

Setting Up Your Kindle Fire

The first time you use your Kindle Fire, you need to go through a series of steps to configure the device:

1. Tap the language you want to use on your device.

2. Tap Continue.

3. Tap the name of your Wi-Fi network.

①

Deutsch

English (United Kingdom)

English (United States)   ✓

Español

Français

Italiano

日本語

Português

简体中文

Continue

②

③ Connect to Wi-Fi

🛜 10 12_EXT

🛜 de ault

🛜 HF -Print-3F-Rossi

🛜 NE TGEAR-1

🛜 Sh ortFlamingo

🛜 Sh ortFlamingo-guest

🛜 Smithers

🛜 Smithers2

⊕ Join Other Network

⟳ Scan Again

Back   Complete Setup Later

4. Enter the password for your Wi-Fi network.

5. Tap Connect.

6. Tap Continue from the Confirm Account screen.

Is Your Kindle Already Registered?

If you ordered your Kindle Fire from your own Amazon account, it is preregistered before Amazon ships the device to you. If you received your Kindle Fire as a gift or purchased it at a retail store, you need to register the device before you can access content.

COMPLETE SETUP LATER

If you're eager to play with your Kindle Fire without having to go through all the setup motions, use the Complete Setup Later option that appears at the bottom of the Connect to a Wi-Fi Network screen. Because this aborts the entire setup process, you must manually go into the My Account option in Settings to register your Kindle Fire with your Amazon account to gain access to the Amazon Cloud. You also must set up a connection in the Wireless option in Settings before you can connect to the Internet. My advice is to be patient and go through the entire setup procedure right away.

>>>Go Further

Connecting to an Unlisted Wi-Fi Network

If your network's name isn't listed on the Connect to Wi-Fi screen, you might need to manually enter the information necessary to connect to your Wi-Fi network. Follow these steps:

1. Tap Join Other Network at the bottom of the network list.

2. Enter the name (SSID) of your network.

3. Tap the type of security that your network uses.

4. Enter the password for your network, if necessary.

5. Tap Save.

Manually Connecting to a Wi-Fi Network

If you need to return to the Wi-Fi setup or want to set up an additional Wi-Fi connection, swipe your finger down from the time at the top of the screen to open the Quick Settings, and then tap Wireless. From the Wireless screen, tap Wi-Fi.

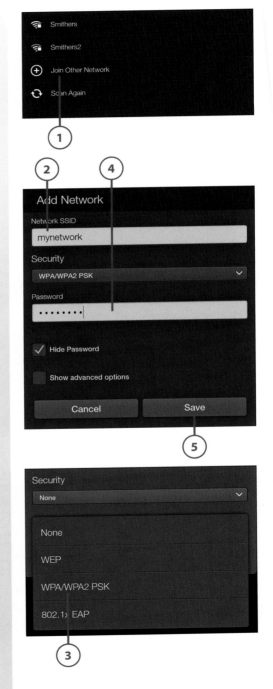

Connecting to Facebook and Twitter

Your Kindle Fire can help you stay connected to your social networks. If you enter your username and passwords during the initial setup, the Facebook and Twitter apps are automatically configured for you.

1. Select Connect Your Facebook Account.

2. Enter your email address.

3. Enter your password.

4. Tap Connect.

5. Repeat steps 1–4 for Twitter.

6. Tap Next to complete the setup process.

You've reached the end of the guided setup. Congratulations! After you complete the initial setup, the Kindle Fire guides you through a series of screens that describe some of the basic usability features of the tablet. And now you're ready to play.

The Home Screen

After you complete the initial setup, the home screen appears. The Carousel contains thumbnails for your books and recently accessed content and websites. Swipe or flick across the Carousel to browse the items available there. Tapping an item opens that item. You can't change the order of items in the Carousel; the most recently accessed items always appear first.

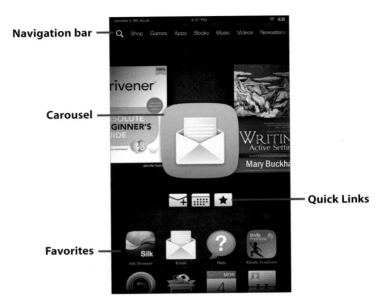

The Navigation bar provides quick access to the various content libraries available on the Kindle Fire. If you select a specific content library, you see content from only that library. Swipe or flick across the Navigation bar to see additional categories of content.

The Quick Links bar appears when you hold your Kindle Fire in portrait mode, providing thumbnails of content related to the item in the center of the Carousel. If the Carousel displays a book at the center, for example, the Quick Links show books that other readers have purchased through Amazon. Some apps provide Quick Links to tasks within that app. If the Carousel is focused on the email app, as shown here, the Quick Links provide options to send a new message or view your Favorite Contacts. If you change the orientation of your device to landscape mode, the Quick Links bar disappears.

Downloading Items

The Carousel displays items both downloaded to your Kindle Fire (called *device items*) and items you've previously purchased that are stored in your online library (called *cloud items*). If you want to open a cloud item, you first need to download it to your device.

1. Swipe to the item you want to download.

2. Tap the item to download it to your device.

3. While the item is downloading, you can tap the X to cancel the download. After an item has been downloaded, it is a device item and can be accessed at any time, even when the Kindle Fire is not connected to the Internet.

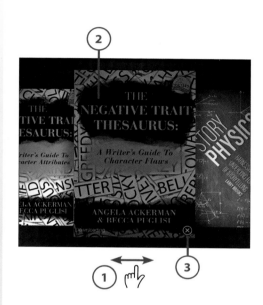

FINDING YOUR ITEMS

>>>Go Further

The Carousel on the home screen shows a mix of cloud and device items, but it shows only the most recently accessed items. If you are looking for content that is not visible on the Carousel, use the Navigation menu to access the type of content you're seeking (books, music, and so on), and then download the item you want from that screen.

Removing Downloaded Items from Your Kindle Fire

After an item is downloaded, it takes up some of the memory on your Kindle Fire. The amount of memory you have available varies by which model of the Kindle Fire you own. You can free up memory by removing unused items from your device. This removes only the device copy of the item; this content is still available to you in your cloud library, so you can download it again at a later date.

1. Tap and hold the item you want to remove.

2. Tap Remove from Device.

Adding an Item to Favorites

Favorites icons appear on the home screen below the Carousel. They provide a convenient way for you to access your most-often-used items. You can add any item to Favorites. If you add more items than can appear on the screen, you can scroll down to view additional items.

1. Tap and hold the item you want to add to Favorites.

2. Tap Add to Home.

3. Your Favorites appear below the Carousel. You can swipe upward to see all your Favorites.

Adding Subscription Items to Favorites

If you add a subscription item to your home screen and that item isn't currently on your device, the item is downloaded immediately. If you remove that item from your device later, it is automatically removed from the home screen, as well. You'll learn more about subscriptions in Chapter 3, "Using Amazon's Manage Your Kindle Page."

Removing an Item from Favorites

If you decide that you no longer want an item to be listed among your Favorites, you can remove it.

1. Tap and hold the item in Favorites.

2. Tap Remove.

3. To remove additional Favorites, tap the item and then tap the Remove button.

4. To return to the home screen, tap the X.

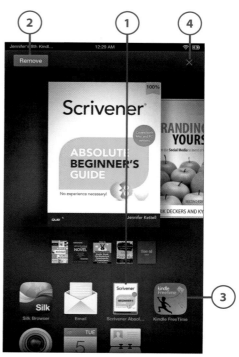

Rearranging Favorites

By default, items are listed in Favorites in the order in which you add them. If you want to rearrange your Favorites, you can easily do so.

1. Tap and hold the item you want to move.

2. Drag the item to the new location.

3. Release the item.

4. Tap the X to return to the home screen.

Navigating the Kindle Fire

By now, you're already familiar with tapping to select buttons and other items on your Kindle Fire. You can also use several other gestures to interact with your Kindle Fire.

Canceling a Tap

Taps are registered when you lift your finger from the screen. If you tap something by mistake and you want to cancel the tap, slide your finger onto another part of the screen before lifting it.

In addition to tapping to select items, you can double-tap to do things such as zoom in on a figure in a book or a website. To do this, tap your finger on the same point on the screen twice in quick succession.

Tap to open

Swipe to scroll

You can scroll through lists of items both horizontally and vertically by swiping your finger. Hold your finger on the list and move it up and down or left and right to scroll through items. To quickly scroll, flick your finger in the direction you want to scroll as you remove your finger from the screen.

To incrementally zoom in and out, you can use pinch and reverse pinch gestures. This is typically used on pictures, websites, and subscription content, but many applications also allow you to use this gesture.

To zoom in, place your thumb and index finger on the screen close together and then move them apart (reverse pinching). To zoom out, place your thumb and index finger on the screen with some distance between them and then move them together (pinching).

Zoom in

Zoom out

Accessing Content Libraries

Use the Navigation bar at the top of the home screen to access content libraries for your books, music, movies, and apps. Content libraries are divided into Cloud and On Device listings. You can also use the libraries to access associated Amazon stores to acquire more content.

1.   Tap a content library in the Navigation bar.

2. Tap Cloud to view cloud content in the selected library or On Device to view device content.

3. Tap Store to view the Amazon store to view or acquire additional content for your Kindle Fire.

4. Tap the Library button to return to the content library.

5. From either the Store or the Library, tap the Home button to return to the home screen.

Opening Navigation Panels

When you tap on one of the content libraries in the Navigation bar, all the content within that library becomes accessible. Each content library has a navigation panel to access additional content or manage that library. The options available from these navigation panels vary by content library.

1. From the Navigation bar, enter a content library, such as Books.

2. Swipe from the left side of the screen toward the right to open the navigation panel. Alternatively, tap the navigation panel icon.

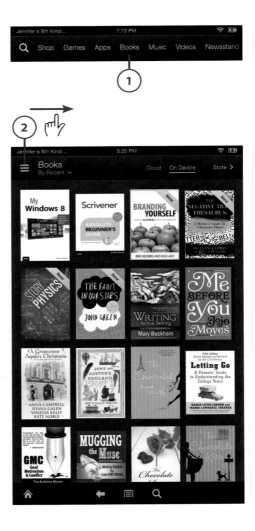

3. To close the navigation panel, swipe from the right side of the panel to the left of the screen. Alternatively, tap the navigation panel icon.

Notifications and Options

The status bar appears at the top of the Kindle Fire screen. It displays the name of your Kindle Fire, a notification indicator (if notifications are present), the clock, the Wi-Fi signal indicator, and the battery meter. If you have the Kindle Fire HDX Wi-Fi + 4G LTE, the status bar also displays the strength of your 4G signal.

Viewing Notifications

Your Kindle Fire uses the notification indicator to inform you of the status of background tasks and let you know when you've received email. When you see the indicator, open the notifications screen to view the message.

1. Swipe the status bar downward to open the notification screen.

2. Tap a notification for more information or additional options.

Using the Options Bar

The Options bar appears at the bottom of the screen in portrait orientation or on the right side of the screen when you hold the device in landscape orientation. The buttons on the Options bar are called icons and include a Home icon, a Back icon, a Menu icon, and a Search icon on most screens. The Home icon always takes you to the home screen. The Back icon takes you back one screen, the Menu icon displays a menu for the current screen, and the Search icon displays the Search screen.

Home   Back Menu Search

Other Options Bar Icons

Depending on the screen, you might see additional icons on the Options bar. These are covered throughout the book, where applicable.

Switching Applications or Content

You can easily switch to another recently used item without returning to the home screen. The Quick Switch bar displays the books, videos, music, and apps that you have most recently opened.

1. Swipe from the Option bar to the middle of the screen.

2. Swipe across the Quick Switch bar to scroll through your recently used content.

3. Tap the item you want to open.

Switching Content in Full Screen

If you're using an app or viewing a web page in full screen, a "nub" appears at the bottom of the screen. Tap on the nub to open the Options bar. Swipe from the nub toward the middle of the screen to open the Options bar and the Quick Switch bar.

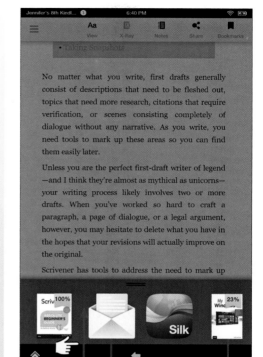

Settings

I cover many of the Kindle Fire's settings throughout the book as necessary, but you should be immediately familiar with some general settings.

Locking the Screen Orientation

When you turn your Kindle Fire while holding it, the screen rotates automatically to match the orientation of the device. In some cases, you might want to prevent the screen from rotating, such as if you're reading in bed and shift to get more comfortable. You can lock the orientation to prevent screen rotation.

1. With the screen displaying the desired orientation, swipe the status bar down to open the Quick Settings.

2. Tap Auto-Rotate to lock the orientation. The label on the icon changes to Locked.

Orientation Isn't Always Your Choice

If you are watching videos, your Kindle Fire automatically switches to landscape orientation. Certain apps also lock the orientation.

Adjusting Screen Brightness

As mentioned earlier, the screen on the Kindle Fire uses more power than anything else, and the brighter the screen, the more battery power it uses. If you want to increase battery life, lower the brightness of the display.

1. Swipe the status bar down to open the Quick Settings.

2. Tap Brightness.

3. Slide the brightness control to the right to increase brightness and to the left to decrease brightness.

Enabling Airplane Mode

Sometimes you need to turn off the Wi-Fi connection on your Kindle Fire, such as when instructed by a flight attendant or in sensitive areas. This is known as Airplane Mode. If you have a Kindle Fire with Wi-Fi + 4G LTE, putting your device into Airplane Mode disables both Wi-Fi and cellular connections.

1. Swipe the status bar down to open the Quick Settings.

2. Tap Wireless.

3. To enable Airplane Mode, tap On. To disable Airplane Mode and reconnect, tap Off.

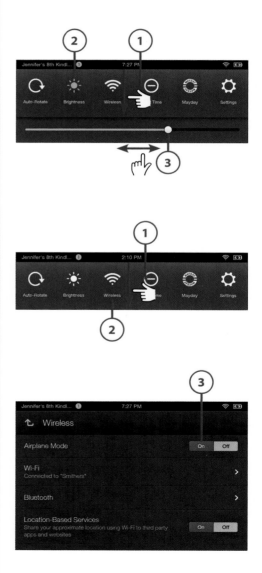

Flying with Your Kindle Fire

Although the FAA has eased restrictions on using electronic devices on airplanes during takeoff and landing, not all airlines are allowing this as of yet. Also, if you have a Wi-Fi + 4G LTE model, be aware that you must still use Airplane Mode to disable your cellular connection during the flight.

Using Quiet Time to Disable Notifications

After you have set up your device for email, Facebook, and other services and social media, you may receive notifications throughout the day. If you do not want to be disturbed, enable Quiet Time to hide these notifications and disable the notification sounds.

1. Swipe the status bar down to open the Quick Settings.

2. Tap Quiet Time. An icon in the status bar indicates that Quiet Time has been enabled.

Quiet Time Is Not Downtime

Your Kindle Fire still collects notifications while Quiet Time is enabled. Your device still checks for new email at the set interval and intercepts social media updates. However, it does not notify you of these messages until you disable Quiet Time. You can also still use the email and social media apps while Quiet Time is enabled.

Changing the Screen Timeout

While you're learning how to use your Kindle Fire, particularly if you are doing each task as you follow along with this book, you might get frustrated if the device automatically goes into sleep mode just as you're about to reach for it. Your Kindle Fire's screen turns off automatically after 5 minutes without use. You can adjust the timeout or completely disable it.

1. Tap the top of the screen (where the name of the device and time are displayed) and drag down.

2. Tap Settings.

3. Tap Display & Sounds.

4. Tap Display Sleep.

5. Select a screen timeout period.

6. Press the Home button to return to the home screen.

Checking Device Information

The Device screen displays information about your Kindle Fire, such as the percentage of battery remaining, how much storage space you've used, the version of your operating system, and other useful information.

1. Swipe the status bar down to open the Quick Settings.

2. Tap Settings.

3. Tap Device.

4. The Device screen displays. If you want to check your storage space, tap Storage.

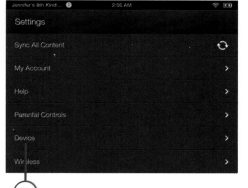

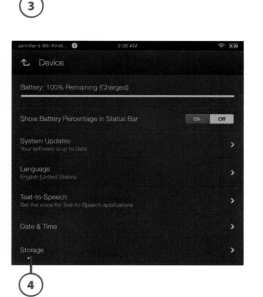

5. The Storage screen displays how much space you have used across various types of data. To view a list of items within each area, tap the arrow to the right of that category.

6. If storage is at a premium, you can remove items from your device. Click the check box to the left of any items you want to remove.

7. Tap Remove to delete the items from your device. Any content you've acquired from Amazon remains available in your cloud storage.

Examining Device Storage

If you look closely at your device storage, you will notice that the total of used space and free space does not equal the total amount of storage you purchased for your device (8GB up to 64GB). This is because the Fire 3.0 operating system itself consumes some of the storage on your device.

Using the Keyboard

Your Kindle Fire's keyboard is much like the keyboard you use on your computer. However, unlike your computer's keyboard, this one has no physical keys. Instead, your Kindle Fire's keyboard uses touch, just like the rest of the interface.

At first, you might find the keyboard a bit hard to get used to, especially if you're typing a lengthy email or document. After some time, however, you'll find it to be an easy way to enter data.

Entering Text

Entering text using your Kindle Fire's keyboard is a simple task, and a few convenient features make it easier.

1. Tap an area where text entry is possible, such as the Silk web browser app. Learn more about Silk in Chapter 12, "Browsing the Web with Silk."

2. Tap letters on the keyboard to enter your text.

3. Tap a suggested word to insert the word.

A Couple of Shortcuts

You can quickly add a period to the end of a sentence by double-tapping the space key. Activate caps lock by double-tapping the Shift key.

Positioning the Cursor

As you type, characters are added at the position of the cursor. You can reposition the cursor, if necessary.

1. Tap in the text entry area.

2. Tap a new position to move the cursor indicator. (You cannot drag the cursor itself.)

Selecting and Editing Text

If you want to change or remove some of the text you've entered, you can select a block of text instead of deleting one character at a time.

1. Double-tap the entered text.

2. Drag the left indicator to the beginning of your desired selection.

3. Drag the right indicator to the end of your desired selection.

4. Press Backspace to delete the selection or type to replace the selection.

Selecting an Entire Block of Text

If you want to select everything you typed into a text area, such as the entire body of an email message, tap Select All above the selection indicators.

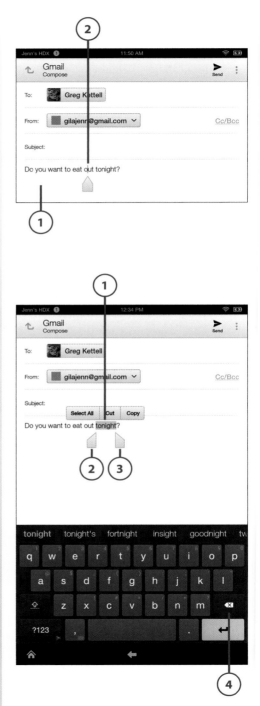

Copying/Cutting and Pasting Text

You might want to copy or cut a selection of text and then paste it somewhere else. You can paste text either within the same message or document or into another message or document.

1. Double-tap the text you want to copy or cut.

2. Drag the indicators to make your selection, or tap Select All.

3. Tap Copy or Cut.

4. Tap and hold where you want to paste the text you copied or cut.

5. Tap Paste.

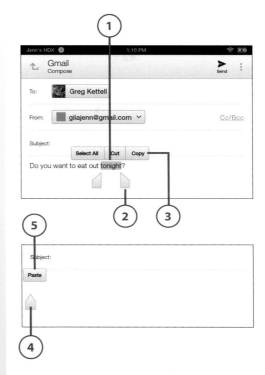

Entering Punctuation and Numbers

The most-often-used punctuation marks appear above the keyboard for easy access while you type. You can use the number keyboard to enter other punctuation, numbers, and symbols.

1. Tap the number key to change the keyboard so that it displays numbers and punctuation marks.

2. Tap the symbols key to change the keyboard so that it displays symbols.

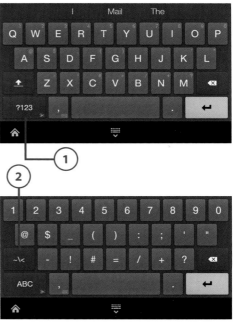

3. Tap a number, a punctuation mark, or a symbol to enter it.

4. Tap the ABC key to return to the alphabet keyboard.

Adding Accent Marks and Diacriticals

If you are typing in a foreign language, you might need to add accent marks and diacriticals to certain letters. The letters that often require these marks are a, e, i, o, u, c, and n.

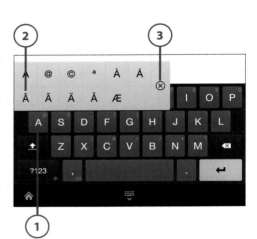

1. Tap and hold a letter that requires an accent.

2. When the diacritical menu pops up, tap the desired character and release.

3. To exit the diacritical menu without selecting a character, tap the X to close the menu.

Splitting the Keyboard

When the device is flat on a table, it's easy to tap away at the keyboard with your fingers. If you're holding the device in your hands, however, you may want to split the keyboard to make it easier to type with your thumbs.

1. Tap and hold the comma (,) key. There is a keyboard symbol at the bottom-right corner of the key.

2. When the keyboard icon appears, release the comma key.

3. To reconnect the keyboard halves, tap and hold the comma key again, and then release it when the keyboard icon appears.

Connecting to Other Hardware

The Kindle Fire is a self-contained device. You can access your content directly from the Kindle Fire without connecting it to a computer or any other hardware. However, you might want to use accessories that will enhance the quality of your interaction with your Kindle Fire. You can pair the Kindle Fire with Bluetooth keyboards, headphones, or speakers.

Adding Bluetooth Accessories

Bluetooth keyboards and headsets can connect wirelessly to your device. With Bluetooth headphones, you can listen to your music without being attached to your Kindle Fire by a wire. A Bluetooth keyboard can help you type messages and documents faster. If you have Bluetooth speakers in your car, you can even play music from your Kindle Fire over your car stereo.

1. Swipe the status bar down to open the Quick Settings.

2. Select Wireless.

3. Select Bluetooth.

4. Tap the On button to enable Bluetooth.

5. Tap Pair a Bluetooth Device.

6. Tap Scan to detect available devices.

7. After the scan is complete, tap the device that you want to pair with.

8. Follow additional instructions, which vary by device.

It's Not All Good

Bluetooth Has Limits

Although Bluetooth microphones and headsets are popular, particularly among gamers, the Kindle Fire does not support these devices. If you want to use voice chat, you must use the Kindle Fire's built-in microphone.

Searches

All the content in your Kindle library is indexed for easy searching. Search is more useful than it might seem at first. For example, when you're reading a novel, you can use search to find references to a particular character. This is especially helpful when you pick up a book that you haven't read in a while.

Search results include content both on your device and in the cloud.

Searching Within Content

You can also search within books and other content. Learn how to do that in the "Searching Content and Accessing Reference Materials" section of Chapter 4, "Reading on the Kindle Fire."

Searching Your Library

Searching your library returns results from books, periodicals, music, documents, and apps.

1. From the home screen, tap the Search icon in the Navigation bar.

2. Tap Libraries to search your library.

3. Enter the text you want to search for using the keyboard that appears at the bottom of the screen. Results appear as you type.

4. Tap the item you want. If the item is on your device, it opens. If the item is stored on the Amazon Cloud, it downloads to your Kindle Fire.

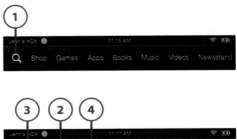

Searching the Web

In addition to searching for items in your libraries, you can search the Web quickly from the home screen.

1. From the home screen, tap the Search icon in the Navigation bar.

2. Tap Web to search the Web.

3. Enter the text you want to search for. Results appear as you type.

4. Tap an item in the results to open a search page using your default search engine. The preset default search engine is Bing.

Changing Your Web Search Engine

Learn how to set your default web search engine in Chapter 12.

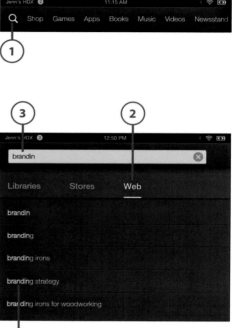

Searching Amazon Stores

You can search for items in the Amazon Stores from the home screen. This is similar to performing a search on the Amazon website, but you can do it right from your Kindle Fire.

1. From the home screen, tap the Search icon in the Navigation bar.

2. Tap Stores to search Amazon Stores.

3. Enter the text you want to search for. Results appear as you type.

4. Tap an option in the results to get a list of items from a particular Amazon Store that matches your search terms.

5. Tap the item you want to see from the list of items.

Getting Help

Although this book attempts to cover all the major features of your Kindle Fire, you may still occasionally find yourself in need of further assistance. The Kindle Fire HDX has several ways for you to get answers to your questions.

The Mayday button provides access to a live customer service representative to answer your questions directly. You can also view the Kindle Fire User Guide on your device. If you want to get answers to your questions or discuss your device with the Kindle user community, the Kindle Help Forums are available online at www.amazon.com/gp/help/customer/forums/kindleqna/.

Using the Mayday Button

Amazon provides 24/7 live customer support directly on your Kindle Fire HDX by way of the Mayday Button. When you are connected, the customer support representative can access your screen and demonstrate exactly how to use features on your device.

1. From the home screen, swipe down to open the Quick Settings.

2. Tap the Mayday button.

3. On the Amazon Assist screen, tap Connect.

4. When the customer service representative appears on the screen, explain your question or problem.

5. Follow the directions given by the customer service representative. He or she may draw on your screen to guide you.

6. When you are finished speaking with the representative, press End.

Accessing the Kindle Fire User Guide

If you prefer not to interact directly with a customer service representative, you can refer to the Kindle Fire User Guide on your device.

1. From the home screen, swipe down to open the Quick Settings.

2. Tap the Mayday button.

3. On the Amazon Assist screen, tap User Guide.

4. In the User Guide, tap a topic to learn more about how to use your Kindle Fire.

5. To search the User Guide, tap the Search icon in the upper-right corner of the screen.

6. Tap the search box and enter a search term. Items in the User Guide matching your search will appear as you type.

7. Tap one of the results to open that topic in the User Guide.

8. When reading certain topics in the User Guide, you may come across links to help you access features on the Amazon site. If you click them, they open in the Silk browser.

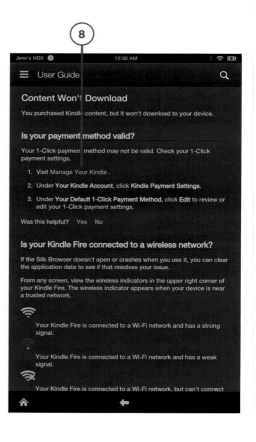

Cloud
Player

Instant
Video

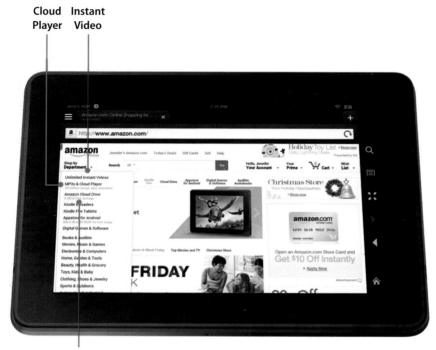

Cloud
Drive

In this chapter, you learn how to load Amazon and other content onto your Kindle Fire and use Amazon's Cloud to access content from your computer. Topics include the following:

→ Amazon Prime
→ Amazon Cloud Drive
→ Amazon Cloud Player
→ Amazon Instant Video
→ Kindle Reader Applications and Kindle Cloud Reader
→ Transferring files from your computer

Accessing Amazon's Cloud Services

Amazon offers a collection of cloud services that augment the functionality of the Kindle Fire. In fact, your Kindle Fire is designed to be a handheld conduit into these cloud services. You can set up the Amazon Cloud Player, add all your music, and have that music immediately available to you on your Kindle Fire anywhere you can connect to the Internet. You can get a movie or TV show from Amazon on your computer or set-top box, watch part of it on your television, and then pick right up to watch the rest on your Kindle Fire while in bed or while traveling. You can also use Amazon's Cloud Services to load your personal photos and documents onto your Kindle Fire. Even if you leave your Kindle Fire behind, all your music, books, videos, and personal files are accessible from any computer with an Internet connection or from many mobile devices.

Amazon Prime

The key to accessing Amazon's Cloud Services is your Amazon account. A standard Amazon account enables you to manage your Kindle Fire device (more on that in Chapter 3, "Using Amazon's Manage Your Kindle Page") and to purchase books, music, and much more. To get the full value from your Kindle Fire, however, consider upgrading to an Amazon Prime account.

An Amazon Prime account costs $79 per year. For that price, you get the following:

- **Prime Instant Videos:** Unlimited, instant streaming of more than 40,000 movies and television shows. You can watch on your Kindle Fire or on any other Internet-connected TV or game machine you own.

- **Kindle Lending Library:** You can check out one book per month from the Kindle Lending Library catalog without any due dates and load it on your Kindle Fire. The Kindle Lending Library has more than 350,000 titles, so you're sure to find something to read each month.

- **Free two-day shipping:** When you shop for material goods on the Amazon site, you get free two-day shipping on most items. One-day shipping costs only $3.99 per item for eligible purchases. The Amazon Store sells everything from toys to food to clothing, so it's easy to see a return on your $79 Prime membership investment if you frequently shop online.

Watch 'The Hunger Games' and thousands of movies and TV episodes for $0.00 with your Prime membership. Browse all videos ›

Your Benefits

FREE Two-Day Shipping
Get free Two-Day Shipping on millions of items

Prime Instant Video
Enjoy unlimited instant streaming of over 41,000 popular movies and TV episodes

Kindle Owners' Lending Library
Borrow one Kindle Book per month from over 350,000 titles for free on any Kindle device with no due dates

Extended Prime Benefits for Caregivers and Students

If you are the primary caregiver (mom, dad, grandparent, and so forth) of a young child, you can get 20 percent off diapers, wipes, and certain other family goods by joining Amazon Mom as a member of Amazon Prime. Browse to www.amazon.com/prime for details.

If you are a college student, you can get a free 6-month subscription to Amazon Prime and then continue for $39 per year, a 50% discount over the regular membership fee.

Setting Up Amazon Prime

When you went through the setup process for your Kindle Fire, you either connected to an existing Amazon account or created a new one. You can set up a free trial of Prime on the same account. You do this on your Kindle Fire using the Silk browser or via the web browser on your computer.

1. Open a web browser and navigate to www.amazon.com.

2. Click Try Prime. If you are not already logged in to your Amazon account, enter your email address and password.

3. Click Start Your 30-Day Free Trial.

4. Enter your billing information.

5. Select Start Your 30-Day Free Trial.

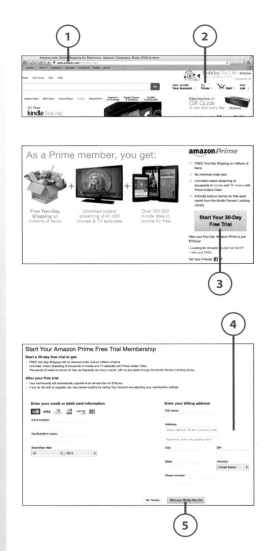

Prime All the Time

At the end of your free trial, Amazon automatically bills you for $79 to extend your Prime membership for a full year. If you decide that you don't want to keep Prime, go to the Amazon.com site, select Your Account, and then select Do Not Upgrade sometime before the end of your 30-day trial.

Amazon Cloud Drive

Your computer has a hard drive in it where you can store your stuff. When you're sitting at your computer, that stuff is easy to access, but what about when you're not at your computer? The cloud is like having a hard drive available from anywhere you have Internet access.

Amazon provides 5GB of free storage that you can use for photos, personal documents, or anything else you want to store in the cloud. This space is in addition to the unlimited cloud storage Amazon provides for books, music, and videos you purchase directly from Amazon. If you need additional storage, Amazon offers plans from 20GB for $10 a year to 1,000GB for $500 a year. As a frame of reference, a typical HD movie is approximately 2GB (2,000MB). A single song is 3MB to 6MB, and a complete album is around 50MB. A high-quality photo is about 2MB to 3MB. As you see, if you start putting all these items onto your cloud storage, it can fill up quickly.

>>>Go Further

WHY WOULD YOU NEED MORE SPACE?

You can use your Amazon Cloud Drive for more than just making your files accessible to your Kindle Fire. Your Cloud Drive can serve as a backup for important files in case your computer crashes. You can also use it to access your files from any other computer with Internet access simply by logging in to your Amazon account.

Content you purchase on Amazon is automatically accessible from your Amazon Cloud account and, thus, from your Kindle Fire. But to access your personal photos and documents, you must upload them to your Cloud Drive.

File and folder management

Upload Files button

Folders

Amount of used storage

Accessing Your Cloud Drive

You can access your Cloud Drive using Silk on your Kindle Fire or using the web browser on your computer.

1. Open your web browser and go to www.amazon.com.

2. Hover over Shop by Department. If you access the Amazon website from Silk, tap Shop by Department.

3. When the Shop by Department menu opens, point to Amazon Cloud Drive.

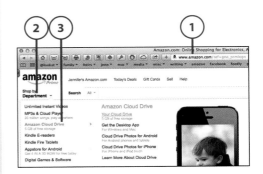

4. Select Your Cloud Drive from the menu. You might get a prompt to install the desktop application, which I explain later in this chapter. You can install it at this time or click Continue to Your Cloud Drive. (Enter your email address and Amazon password, if prompted.)

After you log in, you'll see your Cloud Drive and a big Upload button to get you started. I show you how to create folders and upload files next.

Creating Folders

By default, your Cloud Drive contains folders for the common file types. You'll see folders for pictures, documents, and videos. Those folders are a good starting point, but you might want to create additional folders. For example, if you're uploading pictures of your pets, you might want to first create a folder inside the Pictures folder called Pets and then upload those pictures there.

1. Click New Folder. If you want to place the new folder within another folder, first click that folder from the Folders sidebar.

2. Enter a name for the folder.

3. Click Save Folder.

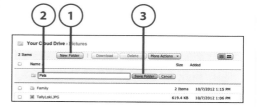

More Actions
You can copy, move, and rename files and folders using the More Actions button.

Deleting Folders

You can delete folders from your Cloud Drive that you no longer need or to free up some space.

1. Click Your Cloud Drive so that your folders are visible.

2. Check the box to the left of the folder(s) you want to delete.

3. Click Delete. You will not see confirmation of this action, so be sure you choose your files correctly.

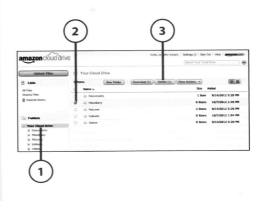

Recovering Deleted Items

If you accidentally delete your files, you can recover them. If you delete a folder that contains files, the files are deleted along with the folder. Recovering a folder also recovers the files that were originally inside the folder.

1. Click Deleted Items.

2. Check the box to the left of the files or folders you want to recover.

3. Click Restore to Folder.

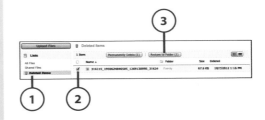

Permanently Deleting Files

When you delete a file or folder, it is moved to a Deleted Items folder and continues to use space in your Cloud Drive. To permanently delete these items, click the Permanently Delete button in Deleted Items.

Adding Files to Your Cloud Drive

To add files to your Cloud Drive, you upload them to Amazon.

1. Click the Upload Files button near the top-left corner of the Cloud Drive screen.

2. Click the drop-down list to select a folder for your uploaded files.

3. Select your folder.

4. Click Select.

5. Click Select Files to Upload, locate the files on your computer, and select them.

After step 1, you might see a notice about the Amazon Cloud Drive application. You can choose to follow the prompts and download this application or proceed uploading your files using your web browser.

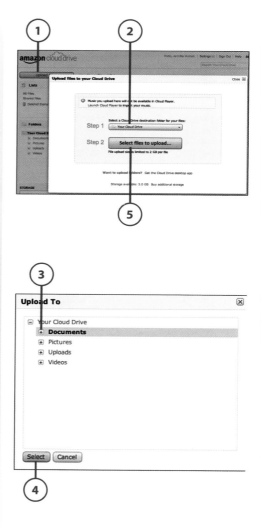

Downloading the Cloud Drive Application

If you use your Cloud Drive on a regular basis, you might find it easier to download and use the Amazon Cloud Drive application. You can download and install it when you see the prompt as you attempt to upload from your web browser, or you can install it at any other time.

1. On your computer, go to www. amazon.com.

2. Hover over the Shop by Department menu.

3. Point to Amazon Cloud Drive.

4. Click Get the Desktop App.

5. On the page that appears, click Free Download. The application downloads to your computer.

6. When the download is complete, double-click the file to initiate the installation procedure and follow the instructions to install the Amazon Cloud Drive application on your computer.

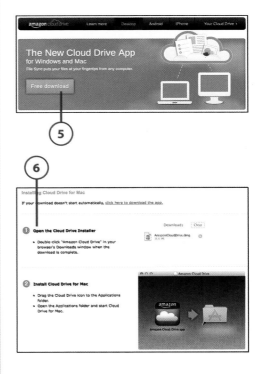

7. Open the Amazon Cloud Drive application and enter your Amazon account username and password.

8. Click Sign In.

9. Click Create Cloud Drive Folder.

Using the Amazon Cloud Drive Application

To add files and folders to your Cloud Drive on a PC, drag files over the Amazon Cloud Drive icon in the taskbar. On a Mac, drag files over the Amazon Cloud Drive icon in the menu bar. On either computer, you can also paste files and folders directly into the Cloud Drive folder that was created earlier in step 9.

Accessing Cloud Drive Files from Your Kindle Fire

Your Kindle Fire automatically syncs with your Cloud Drive whenever you have an Internet connection. Files on your Cloud Drive are automatically sorted into the appropriate content library on the Kindle Fire. If you want to view the photos you uploaded to your Cloud Drive, for example, you can find them in Photos. Personal documents are found in the Docs library.

1. Use the Navigation menu to access the library for the files you want to view. In this example, we access the Docs library.

2. Press the Cloud button if it's not already selected.

3. View a list of the files you have in the cloud for that library.

Folders and Subfolders

Folders and subfolders keep your documents organized. When you view your Docs library By Name, By Recent, or By Type, all your documents are listed, no matter how they're grouped in your Cloud Drive. View your docs By Folder to see only documents within a particular folder or subfolder.

Saving Files to Your Device

When you select a document from the Docs library on your Kindle Fire, it is automatically saved onto your device, and you can then open it from either the Cloud or On Device options. The process for transferring photos from your Cloud Drive onto your device is a bit different.

1. Select Photos from the Navigation bar.

2. Select a photo or folder from the Cloud library.

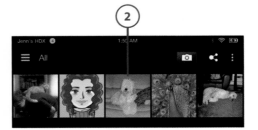

3. Tap the menu icon.

4. Select Download.

Amazon Cloud Player

Amazon Cloud Player is a convenient way to manage music on your Cloud Drive. You can also use it to listen to your music when you don't have your Kindle Fire with you, because it is available from any computer with Internet access or on most mobile devices.

Your Music

Album

Songs

Play controls   Now Playing

Launching Cloud Player

You can also elect to download the Amazon Cloud Player application onto your PC or Mac.

1. Open your web browser and go to www.amazon.com.

2. Point to MP3s & Cloud Player on the menu.

3. Click Play Your Music at Home.

4. Click Download for PC and Mac.

5. When the download is complete, double-click the file to initiate the installation procedure and follow the instructions to install the Amazon Cloud Player app on your computer.

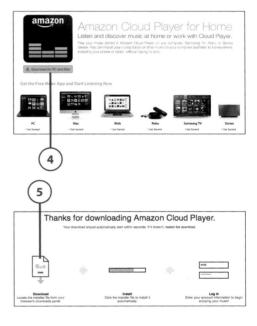

6. Open the Amazon Cloud Player application and enter your Amazon account username and password.

7. Click Sign In.

Amazon Cloud Player Is Also on the Web

You can also access Amazon Cloud Player from your web browser at www.amazon.com/cloudplayer.

Importing Your Music

You can easily upload your music from iTunes and other music apps to Amazon Cloud Player, which then makes it available on your Kindle Fire. You can upload up to 250 songs for free or upgrade to a Premium account that stores up to 250,000 songs for $24.99 a year.

1. Open the Amazon Cloud Player app.

2. In the menu bar, click File, Import Music to Cloud Library.

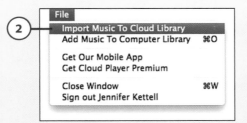

3. Click Continue to launch the Cloud Player website.

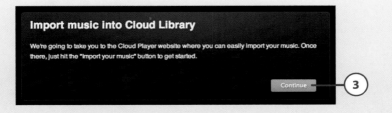

4. Click Import Your Music.

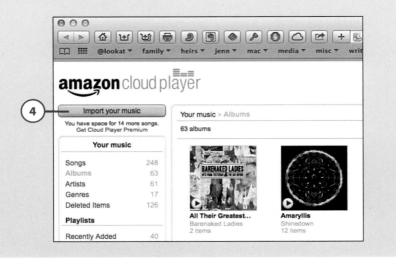

5. Click the Download Now button to download the Amazon Music Importer application, and follow the installation instructions.

6. Open the Amazon Music Importer application, and enter your Amazon account information.

7. Press Sign In Using Our Secure Server.

8. Click Start Scan. The Amazon Music Importer application scans your hard drive, including your iTunes folders (if you have one), for music.

9. After the scan is complete, you might be prompted to choose to upgrade to Cloud Player Premium for $24.99 a year or to select up to 250 songs free. If you have previously imported songs to your Amazon Cloud Player, the number of free songs remaining in your limit appears on the Import button.

10. To select which songs to import into your Cloud Player, check the boxes to the left of the song, album, artist, or playlist title.

11. Click Import Selected.

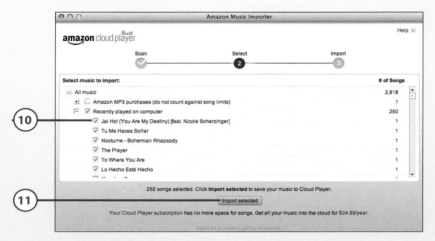

12. When the import is finished, click Close.

Importing Directory from the Cloud Player Website

You can bypass steps 1–3 by opening your browser and navigating directly to www.amazon.com/cloudplayer.

Music that you purchase directly from Amazon's MP3 Store is automatically added to your Amazon Cloud Player, which makes it almost instantly available on your Kindle Fire. It also does not count against the 250 song or Premium storage limitation on your Amazon account.

CONVERTING YOUR MUSIC

The Amazon Cloud Player can import music in either MP3 or unprotected AAC (iTunes) format. If your music is in some other format, you can find free converters by searching the Internet.

Playing Music on Your Computer

You can stream music from the Cloud Player app without downloading the music to your computer.

1. Locate the music you want to play. You can browse by song, album, artist, or genre.

2. Double-click an album to see all the songs on that album.

3. Double-click the song you want to play. You can also press the Play button at the top of the list to play all the songs that are displayed.

4. To play the songs in a list in a random order, press the Shuffle button.

5. To pause the song that is playing, click the Pause button. To continue playing, press the Play button that appears in its place.

6. To go to the next song, click the Next button.

7. To go to the previous song, click the Previous button.

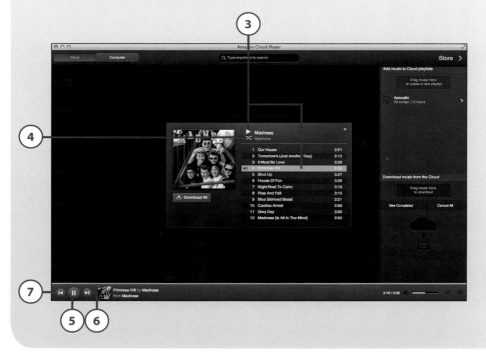

Creating Playlists

You can create playlists of songs to play only the songs you want to hear. Playlists are a great way to make a song list for a party or special event. Playlists you create in Cloud Player are also available on your Kindle Fire.

1. In the Amazon Cloud Player app, drag the songs you want to add to a playlist to the playlist sidebar.

2. Enter a name for the playlist.

3. Click Save.

4. Browse to other songs and drag them to your playlist as desired.

5. Click the Back button when you've completed your playlist.

Refreshing Cloud Drive

Your Cloud Drive refreshes on your Kindle Fire every 10 minutes. Songs or playlists that you add appear after a refresh. If you're in a hurry to get your songs or playlists onto your Kindle Fire, swipe down from the status bar on your Kindle Fire to open the Quick Settings, and then tap Settings and Sync All Content.

Downloading Songs to Your Kindle Fire

If you plan to be away from an Internet connection, you can still play your music by first downloading it to your Kindle Fire.

1. On the Navigation bar of your Kindle Fire, press Music.

2. In the Cloud tab, select a playlist, artist, album, or song.

3. Click the Download All button.

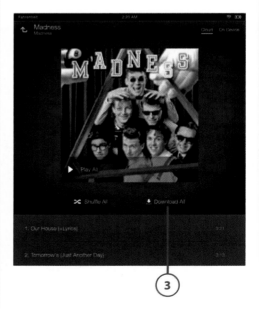

4. If you want to exclude some songs for an artist or album from being downloaded, select the X to the right of the song title. When the download is complete, press Device to confirm that only the music you wanted is now stored on your Kindle Fire.

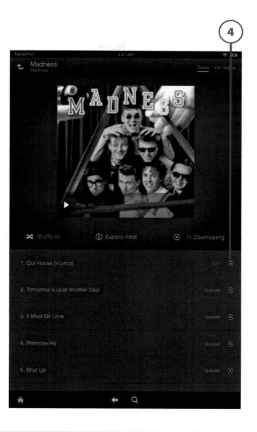

DOWNLOADING MUSIC TO YOUR COMPUTER

The Amazon Cloud Player app detects whether you have iTunes installed on your computer. If you do, after it downloads a song, it automatically imports that song into iTunes. This saves you the trouble of importing music you purchase on Amazon into your iTunes library. If you don't like this behavior, you can change it. You can also change the folder where Amazon Cloud Player saves the songs you download.

To change these settings, click File, Preferences (on a Mac, click Amazon Cloud Player, Preferences). Click the Change button to select a new folder in which to save your downloaded music. Under Export New Amazon MP3

Purchases To, select None if you don't want your Amazon music automatically imported into iTunes.

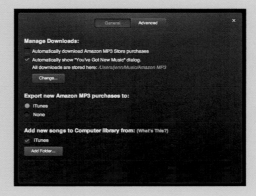

Changing these settings is best done before you start downloading a lot of songs, so you don't have to make a lot of manual changes after the fact.

Amazon Instant Video

Amazon has a huge selection of videos, including both movies and television programs, that you can watch on your Kindle Fire. You can also watch those videos on your computer. You can even purchase or rent videos on your computer and watch them on your Kindle Fire, or vice versa.

When you rent or purchase a video, it becomes available on any computers and devices that are connected to your Amazon account. To view free Prime Instant Videos, however, you must order them directly from the computer or device on which you want to watch them.

Getting Videos from Amazon Instant Video

You can use your computer to buy, rent, or stream Amazon Instant Video. Videos that you buy or rent are available on your computer, on your Kindle Fire, or on any other device that supports Amazon Instant Video.

1. Open your web browser and go to www.amazon.com/instant-video. Or go to www.amazon.com and select Unlimited Instant Videos from the Shop by Department menu; then click Amazon Instant Video Store.

2. Select the movie or TV show that you want to watch.

3. Choose to purchase, rent, or watch your video. Not all options are available for all titles.

Watching Prime Instant Videos Offline

When you purchase or rent a video, you can download it to your computer or device for offline viewing, but you cannot watch free Prime Instant Videos on your computer if you're offline. The Kindle Fire HDX, however, allows you to download select Prime Instant Videos so you can watch them later, even when you're not connected to the Internet. This feature is not available for all Prime Instant Videos. Learn more in Chapter 6, "Watching Video on Your Kindle."

Kindle Reader Applications and Kindle Cloud Reader

In addition to reading on your Kindle Fire, Amazon offers free Kindle Reading apps for the PC, the Mac, and most mobile and tablet devices. All these applications enable you to access your Kindle books from the Amazon Cloud and save them to your computer or device to read offline. You can also access your Kindle books from the Kindle Cloud Reader on the Internet. If you purchase new books from the Kindle Store while on your computer or mobile/tablet device, it appears in your Cloud account so you can also read it on your Kindle Fire.

Accessing Kindle Reader Applications

Before you can read Kindle books on your computer, tablet, or smartphone, you must download and install the appropriate app.

1. In a web browser, go to www.amazon.com.

2. In the Shop By Department menu, choose Kindle E-readers, and then choose Free Kindle Reading Apps.

3. Select your computer or device and follow the directions for downloading and installing the appropriate app.

Downloading Smartphone and Tablet Apps

The information pages for each of the smartphone and tablet apps (iPhone and iPod Touch, Android, Windows Phone, BlackBerry, iPad, Android Tablet, and Windows 8 tablet) have links to the appropriate store or marketplace to download the required application.

Accessing Kindle Cloud Reader

The Kindle Cloud Reader makes it possible to read your Kindle books in your web browser from any location with Internet access. Kindle Cloud Reader requires a current version of either Google Chrome (www.google.com/chrome), Apple Safari (www.apple.com/safari), or Firefox (www.getfirefox.com). It does not run on Microsoft Internet Explorer.

1. Browse to read.amazon.com using your web browser. You can also go to www.amazon.com, choose Kindle from the Shop by Department menu, and then select Kindle Cloud Reader.

2. Click the Get Started Now button.

3. Enter your email address and Amazon password, and then click Sign In.

4. View your Kindle Library in your browser window.

Cloud button shows books in the Cloud

Downloaded button displays books you've downloaded to your computer

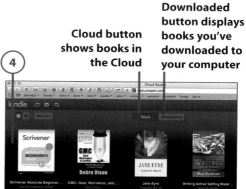

Opening and Downloading Books

When you select a book, the Kindle Reader app or Amazon Cloud Reader automatically begins downloading it to your device or computer. This makes the book available even if you continue reading offline.

1. Locate the book you want to read. You can click the magnifying glass at the top of the screen to search for books, if necessary.

2. Click a book to start reading it. If you are using the Kindle Cloud Reader, the book begins downloading to your computer as you read. If you are using one of the other Kindle Reader apps, the book downloads to your device and then allows you to read it.

3. If you want to download a book without immediately beginning to read in the Kindle Cloud Reader and computer Kindle Reader apps, right-click the book and click Download & Pin Book. In the smartphone and tablet Kindle Reader apps, press and hold the book until a Download button appears; then press that button.

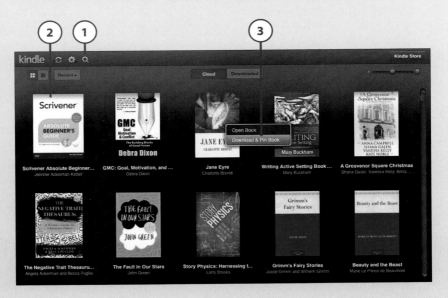

Reading Books on the Kindle Cloud Reader

The Kindle Cloud Reader has many features to make reading a book more enjoyable. The other Kindle Reader applications are similar but might have slight differences in the location and method for accessing some features.

1. Open a book as described in the previous section. If the book has been opened previously on any Kindle device, it automatically opens at the farthest point read.

2. To turn pages, use the arrow keys on your keyboard or click the arrows on the left and right sides of the page.

3. Quickly access a part of the book using the Go To menu.

4. Change font size, margins, and color settings using the View Settings button.

5. Bookmark a page using the Bookmark button.

6. View notes and highlights using the Show Notes and Marks button.

7. Synchronize with your other Kindle devices using the Synchronize button.

8. Click the Library button to return to your library.

9. See where you are in the book using the location bar.

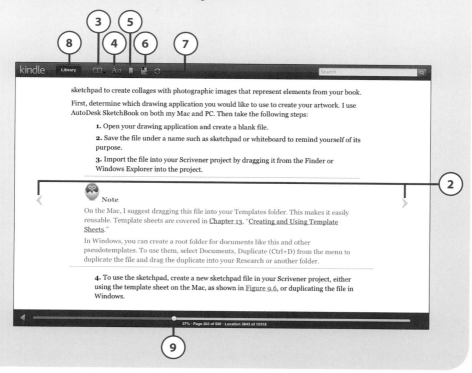

10. To add Notes or Highlights, use your mouse to select the passage you want to mark; then right-click and choose to create a Note or Highlight.

11. To bookmark a page to return to it later, tap the Bookmark icon in the top-right corner of the page.

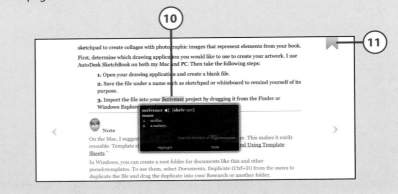

Transferring Files from Your Computer

Most of the content you view on your Kindle Fire is available directly from Amazon and can be easily accessed from the Amazon Cloud. You can also transfer books, videos, music, and other files from additional online sources or your personal library. This is known as *sideloading*. To get this content onto your Kindle Fire, transfer the files via the micro-USB cable that came with your device.

Kindle File Types

You can transfer the following types of files onto your Kindle Fire:

- **Books and documents:** AZW, TXT, PDF, MOBI, PRC, DOC, and DOCX formats
- **Audio (Music):** MP3, Non-DRM AAC (.m4a), MIDI, OGG, and WAV formats
- **Video:** MP4 format
- **Images:** JPEG, GIF, PNG, and BMP formats

The Kindle Fire cannot read Mobipocket files that utilize Digital Rights Management (DRM) protection. The Kindle Fire also does not support EPUB books.

Transferring Files from a PC

If you're using Windows Vista or later, the Kindle Fire automatically shows up as an available external USB drive. After connecting your Kindle Fire to your PC using the micro-USB cable, follow these steps:

1. In Windows Explorer, click Computer.

2. Click Kindle.

3. Double-click Internal Storage.

4. Copy your files from their original location on your PC into the appropriate folders in the Internal Storage folder.

Transferring Files from a Mac

If you're using a Mac, you must download Android File Transfer, a free app, before you can transfer files using USB.

1. In your web browser, go to www.android.com/filetransfer.

2. Click the Download Now button, and follow the instructions to install Android File Transfer to your Applications folder.

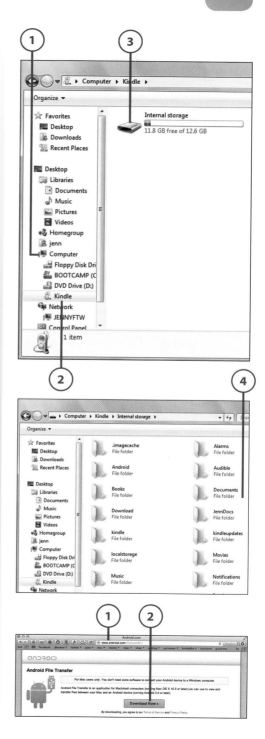

3. Use the micro-USB cable to connect your Kindle Fire to your Mac.

4. Double-click the Android File Transfer app to open it. After you've opened it for the first time, it automatically opens whenever you connect your Kindle Fire to your Mac.

5. Copy your files from their original location on your Mac into the appropriate folders in the Android File Transfer app.

TRANSFERRING FILES FROM LINUX

If you're a Linux user, you can transfer files to your Kindle Fire using a Media Transfer Protocol (MTP) USB driver. You can find more information about connecting your device using MTP at http://research.jacquette.com/jmtpfs-exchanging-files-between-android-devices-and-linux/.

>>>Go Further

Manage content

Manage your library

Manage devices and your account

https://www.amazon.com/ap/digital/fiona/manage?ie=UTF8&ref_=gno_yam_myk#All

@lookat ▾   family ▾   heirx ▾   jenn ▾   mac ▾   media ▾   misc ▾   writing ▾   amazon   facebook   feedly   pin it

amazon *Prime*

Holiday Toy List · Shop now
Presented by Citi

Recommendations   Today's Deals   Gift Cards   Sell   Help

Shop by Department ▾   Search   Kindle Store ▾   Go

Hello, Jennifer
Your Account ▾   Your Prime ▾   Cart ▾   Wish List ▾

Buy a Kindle   Kindle eBooks   Advanced Search   Daily Deals   Free Reading Apps   Kindle Singles   Newsstand   Accessories   Discussions   Manage Your Kindle   Kindle Support

Your Account > Manage Your Kindle

Kindle Help ▾

Your Kindle Library
- All Items
- Books
- Newspapers
- Magazines
- Blogs
- Personal Documents
- Audible Audiobooks
- Active Content
- Your Apps
- Amazon Instant Videos
- Pending Deliveries [19]

Your Kindle Account
- Manage Your Devices
- Subscription Settings
- Kindle Payment Settings
- Personal Document Settings
- Country Settings
- Kindle FreeTime Settings
- Manage Whispercast Membership
- Your Amazon Local Vouchers
- Whispersync Device Synchronization
- Automatic Book Update
- Language Optimized Storefront

Automatic Book Update is now available. **Learn more**

Your Kindle Library

View: [All Items]   OR   Search your library   Go

Showing 1 - 15 of 888 Items

Title	Author	Date ▾	
The Reluctant Traveller: France and the French	Byron, Patrick	November 13, 2013	Actions... ▾
Europe: 40 Amazing Experiences	Lonely Planet	November 13, 2013	Actions... ▾
Russian History, Culture and Judaism	Tafero, Arthur H	November 13, 2013	Actions... ▾
True Irish Ghost Stories	Seymour, St. John D. (St. John Drelincourt)	November 13, 2013	Actions... ▾
Wading Home: A Novel of New Orleans	Story, Rosalyn	November 13, 2013	Actions... ▾
Ye Olde Britain: Best Historical Experiences (Regional Travel Guide)	Lonely Planet	November 13, 2013	Actions... ▾
The History of England, Volume I From the Invasion of Julius Caesar to the Revolution in 1688	Hume, David	November 13, 2013	Actions... ▾
The Grimm Diaries Prequels volume 1- 6: Snow White Blood Red, Ashes to Ashes & Cinder to Cinder, Beauty Never Dies, Ladle Rat Rotten Hut, Mary Mary Quite Contrary, Blood Apples	Jace, Cameron	November 13, 2013	
Stupidly Easy Paleo: Quick and Easy Paleo Recipes the Whole Family Will Love (Quick and Easy Gluten Free Recipes)	Tabakova, Vesela	November 13, 2013	Actions... ▾
The Legends of King Arthur and His Knights	Knowles, Sir James	November 13, 2013	Actions... ▾
The Art of War	Sunzi	November 13, 2013	Actions... ▾
First Position	Lane, Prescott	November 13, 2013	Actions... ▾

In this chapter, you learn how you can use Amazon's Manage Your Kindle page to keep track of your books and subscriptions and manage your payment and device information. Topics include the following:

→ Managing your books and docs
→ Managing subscriptions
→ Updating Kindle payment information
→ Managing your Kindle devices

Using Amazon's Manage Your Kindle Page

Amazon's Manage Your Kindle page is a one-stop location for managing your Kindle content and your Kindle device. If you have multiple Kindle devices, the Manage Your Kindle Page is even more useful.

You can use the Manage Your Kindle page to send books from your Kindle library to any of your Kindle devices. You can also use it to see the periodicals you subscribe to, and you can manage those subscriptions as well. Links enable you to manage your method of payment to Amazon so that items you purchase on your Kindle Fire get charged to the right credit card. Finally, you can register and deregister Kindles and rename your devices from the Manage Your Kindle page.

Managing Your Books and Documents

You can view all the books and documents in your library using Manage Your Kindle. You can also transfer them to your Kindle. Ebooks that you have purchased from Amazon's Kindle Store appear in the Books content library. ebooks that you have purchased from a source other than Amazon appear in the Personal Documents content library. Docs that you see listed in Manage Your Kindle have been emailed to your kindle.com email address for document conversion. Manage Your Kindle doesn't list docs that you load to your Kindle Fire using the micro-USB cable (a process known as *sideloading*).

What's Up with Docs?

When I talk about "docs," I'm talking about Kindle Personal Documents. I use the term *docs* because it is how the Kindle Fire refers to that content library on the device. The Manage Your Kindle page on the Amazon site, however, uses the term Personal Documents.

Chapter 10, "Managing Your Personal Documents and Data," covers docs in detail.

Accessing Manage Your Kindle

Manage Your Kindle is a web page that you access using the web browser on your computer or using Silk on your Kindle Fire.

1. In your web browser, go to www.amazon.com.

2. Hover over the Your Account drop-down menu. If you are accessing the Amazon site from the Silk browser on your Kindle Fire, tap instead of hovering.

3. Choose Manage Your Kindle. If prompted, log in using your email address and Amazon password.

A Faster Way to Manage Your Kindle

You can get to the Manage Your Kindle page directly by going to www.amazon.com/manageyourkindle in your web browser.

Viewing Books and Docs

Manage Your Kindle's default view lists all the books, magazines, subscriptions, apps, and personal docs on your Kindle devices. This section covers books and docs, and I talk about handling newspapers and magazines in the next section.

From the Manage Your Kindle page, you can select the type of content you want to view using the View drop-down list. You can sort content by title, author, or date by clicking one of the column headers. The first click of a column header sorts in descending order; clicking the same column header again sorts that column in ascending order.

Select a content type	Search for a title or author	Change the sort order

Your Kindle Library

View: ✓ All Items   OR   Search your library (GO)

Showing:
- Books
- Newspapers
- Magazines
- Blogs
- Personal Documents
- Audible Audiobooks
- Active Content
- Your Apps
- Amazon Instant Videos

- Kindle FreeTime Library
- Brian's Kindle FreeTime Library
- Amanda's Kindle FreeTime Library
- Loans
- Available for Update

Title	Author	Date ▼
French	Byron, Patrick	November 13, 2013
	Lonely Planet	November 13, 2013
	Tafero, Arthur H	November 13, 2013
	Seymour, St. John D. (St. John Drelincourt)	November 13, 2013
	Story, Rosalyn	November 13, 2013
nces (Regional Travel Guide)	Lonely Planet	November 13, 2013
The History of England, Volume I From the Invasion of Julius Caesar to the Revolution in 1688	Hume, David	November 13, 2013
The Grimm Diaries Prequels volume 1- 6: Snow White Blood		

If you want to see details on an item, click the plus sign next to the item title. If you have a lot of content and you want to search for a particular item, enter a search term and click Go.

Why Use Manage Your Kindle?

A lot of the functionality in Manage Your Kindle, such as transferring a book from the Amazon Cloud to your device, can be accomplished directly on your Kindle Fire. However, if you want to lend a book to another Kindle user (as explained in Chapter 4, "Reading on the Kindle Fire") or permanently delete a book from your Kindle Library, you accomplish those tasks through Manage Your Kindle. It's also a convenient way to deliver content to multiple Kindle devices or apps on your account or to manage your account when someone else in the family is using your Kindle Fire.

Sending Books and Docs to Your Kindle

You can send books and docs to a Kindle device or to the Kindle apps for Android, iPad, iPhone, and iPod Touch. You can send books, but not docs, to the other Kindle apps. Content is delivered within a minute, assuming you are connected to Wi-Fi.

Kindle Apps

When I mention Kindle apps in this chapter, I'm not talking about apps installed on your Kindle Fire. I'm talking about the Kindle app that you can use on a computer, tablet, or smartphone to read Kindle ebooks.

1. Locate the book or doc that you want to send to your Kindle.

2. Hover over (or tap, on the Silk browser) the Actions drop-down list.

3. Click Deliver to My.

4. Select the device from the drop-down list. If the doc you are sending to your Kindle isn't in a format supported by a particular device, that device is not available in the drop-down list.

5. Click Deliver.

Downloading Books to a Computer

You can also download books (but not docs) to your computer. After you download a book, you can side-load it to your Kindle Fire using the micro-USB cable.

1. Hover over (or tap) the Actions drop-down list.

2. Click Download & Transfer via USB.

3. Select the Kindle to which you plan to transfer the book.

4. Click Download and save the book using your browser's download option.

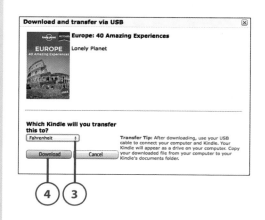

Deleting Books and Docs

You can delete books and docs from your library if you do not want to reread them. Use this feature with caution because doing so removes the item permanently. If you delete a book that you purchased from Amazon, you have to buy it again if you change your mind.

1. Point to the Actions drop-down list.

2. Click Delete from Library.

3. Click Yes to confirm that you want to permanently delete the book from your library.

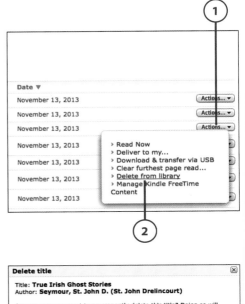

Changing Your Kindle Email Address

Use your Kindle email address to send docs directly to your Kindle. You can change the email address for your Kindle Fire on the Manage Your Kindle page.

1. Click Personal Document Settings.

2. Click Edit next to the Kindle email address you want to change.

3. Enter the new email address.

4. Click Update.

Edit Send-to-Kindle E-mail Address ⊠

Edit the Send-to-Kindle e-mail address used to send personal documents to this Kindle.

Send-to-Kindle E-mail Address: [jennimuse] @kindle.com

[Update] [Cancel]

④   ③

Adding an Approved Email for Docs

To prevent spam on your Kindle device, Amazon delivers only docs emailed from an approved list of senders. You can add an approved email address using Personal Documents Settings.

1. From Personal Documents Settings, click Add a New Approved Email Address in the Approved Personal Document Email List section.

2. Enter the email address you want to approve. You can also enter a partial email address, such as @yourcompany.com, to allow all senders from that particular domain.

3. Click Add Address.

Deleting an Approved Email Address

You can delete an approved email address by clicking Delete to the right of the email address on the Approved Personal Document Email List.

>>>Go Further

PUTTING YOUR KINDLE EMAIL ADDRESS TO WORK

Some non-Amazon online bookstores, such as www.omnilit.com, deliver purchases directly to your Kindle account if you provide them with your Kindle email address. Be sure to add these providers to your approved email list and follow the bookstore site's instructions about adding your Kindle address to your bookstore account before making a purchase.

Disabling Doc Archiving

By default, docs that are sent to your Kindle are also saved in your Kindle library. Amazon gives you 5GB of space for personal doc archiving. You can disable the archiving of personal docs.

1. From Personal Document Settings, click Edit in the Personal Document Archiving section.

2. Deselect the box to disable archiving.

3. Click Update.

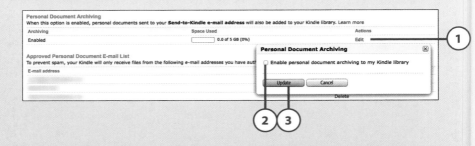

Double the Docs Space

The 5GB of personal doc storage in your Kindle library is separate from the 5GB of storage on your Amazon Cloud Drive, which you can also use for docs (among other files). I recommend saving the Kindle personal doc space for ebook purchases from other bookstores because it is email accessible. Use your Amazon Cloud Drive to store your other personal documents. This has the added benefit of keeping all your truly personal docs together on the Amazon Cloud Drive, which makes them easier to manage and organize.

Managing Subscriptions

You can also manage your magazine and newspaper subscriptions from the Manage Your Kindle page. You can choose which device gets your subscription automatically, send past issues to your Kindle Fire, or download past issues so that you can sideload them to your Kindle Fire. Finally, you can cancel your subscription altogether. To learn more about subscribing to periodicals, see Chapter 4.

Changing Where a Subscription Is Delivered

You choose which device receives the automatic delivery of subscription content when you first subscribe. If you subscribe from your Kindle Fire, it automatically receives the subscription. You can change that choice from Manage Your Kindle. This option is available only if you have multiple Kindle devices registered.

1. Click Subscription Settings.
2. Click Edit for the subscription you want to change.
3. Select a device to which new editions should be delivered.
4. Click Update.

Canceling a Subscription

Subscriptions are automatically charged on a monthly basis, even if the magazine arrives on your Kindle Fire on a different distribution schedule. If you want to cancel a subscription, you can do it from Manage Your Kindle.

1. From Subscription Settings, click Actions for the subscription you want to cancel.

2. Click Cancel Subscription.

3. Select one or more reasons for canceling.

4. Enter a comment if you select Other.

5. Click Cancel Subscription.

Access to Past Issues for Canceled Subscriptions

If you cancel a subscription, any issues that have been downloaded to your Kindle Fire remain in your library. However, you won't be able to download any past issues. Be sure you've downloaded all the issues for which you've paid before you cancel.

Reactivating a Canceled Subscription

Amazon maintains a list of all your inactive subscriptions. You can use this list to easily reactivate a canceled subscription.

1. From Subscription Settings, click View Inactive Subscriptions.

2. Click Actions for the subscription you want to reactivate.

3. Click Reactivate Subscription.

4. Click Reactivate Subscription in the confirmation dialog box.

Why Is the Actions Button Missing?

If you have deregistered the Kindle to which an active subscription was being delivered, the Actions button is missing. Before you can reactivate the subscription, you first need to select a Kindle to which the subscription should be delivered.

It's Not All Good

Resubscribing During the Free Trial

Subscriptions typically begin with a free trial period, during which you receive one or more issues. If you do nothing after the free trial, you are automatically billed the monthly rate. If you cancel a subscription during the free trial and then resubscribe, however, you are billed immediately.

Changing Subscription Privacy Settings

Amazon does not share your email address with content providers unless you explicitly give permission to do so. You can do that using subscription privacy settings.

1. From Subscription Settings, locate Privacy Preferences for Newspapers and Magazine Subscriptions.

2. Click Edit for the subscription you want to modify.

3. Check the box(es) for the information you want to share with the content provider.

4. If you want your settings to be the default for future subscriptions, check the appropriate box.

5. Click Update.

Privacy Preferences for Newspapers and Magazine Subscriptions
Choose which information is shared with publishers for marketing purposes. **Learn more about Privacy**

Title	E-mail address	Use name and billing address for marketing purposes
Cook's Illustrated		Edit
Foreign Affairs		Edit
Newsweek		Edit

View inactive sub

Your Amazon Pri

Kindle Owners' L

Manage Prime Mem

Know Us

Privacy Settings   ⊠

Allow **Cook's Illustrated** to use the following information for marketing purposes.

☐ Name and billing address

☐ E-mail address

   Note: It may take up to 60 days for e-mail changes to take effect

☐ Use these settings for future newspaper and magazine purchases.

[Update]   [Cancel]

Updating Kindle Payment Information

You can change the credit card that Amazon uses for purchases and for current subscriptions.

Changing Amazon Purchases Credit Cards

When you buy Kindle books and MP3s, and rent or purchase Amazon videos, the credit card used for 1-Click purchases at Amazon.com is billed automatically. You can change this credit card information, add a new credit card, or choose a different credit card using Manage Your Kindle.

Multiple Credit Cards

Amazon can store several cards for your account, and you can choose which one is used for your 1-Click purchases on the Manage Your Kindle page. Keep in mind that changing your credit card does not change the credit card used for your subscriptions; you must change those separately.

1. Click Kindle Payment Settings.

2. Click Edit.

3. Enter your new credit card information, or select a different card.

4. Click Continue.

Changing Current Subscriptions Credit Cards

You must individually update payment options for current subscriptions.

1. From Kindle Payment Settings, click Edit for the subscription you want to change.

Kindle Payment Settings

All Kindle transactions are completed with 1-Click. Changes made to your default 1-Click method will apply to future Amazon.com 1-Click transactions, but will not change your current active subscriptions.

Your Default 1-Click Payment Method

Billing Method

MasterCard ***   Edit ——————①

Current Subscriptions

Title ▼	Billing Amount	Payment Method	Actions
Time	$0.00 Daily		Edit Payment
Wired	$0.00 Yearly		Edit Payment

2. Enter the new credit card information.

3. Click Continue.

Your Payment Settings for Cook's Illustrated

Changes that you make to your credit card for this subscription will take effect in your next billing date.

Please select a payment method
Please click the button corresponding to your selection, then fill in all required information.

Continue ●

Pay with existing card	Credit Card No.	Cardholder's Name	Expiration Date
⊙ MasterCard			03 : 2015 :
Pay with new card	Credit Card No.	Cardholder's Name	Expiration Date
② — ○ Amazon.com Visa :			-- : ---- :

Note: Amazon.com Store Cards do not expire

Continue ●——③

It's Not All Good

Updating Credit Card Information

Whenever you change your payment information, you need to remember to update each of your subscriptions, as well. If you have multiple subscriptions, this can be a time-consuming process, and one easily forgotten when you change your 1-Click account.

Managing Your Kindle Devices

You can add multiple Kindles to your account. Having two or more Kindles registered to the same account is useful if you and other family members have the same tastes in books. If you buy a book on one Kindle, you can read it on another Kindle at the same time without having to buy it again.

The Manage Your Devices page lists all your Kindle devices (including any Kindle apps installed on your computer, tablet, or phone). You can deregister a Kindle or change your Kindle's name.

Deregistering a Kindle or Kindle App

If you decide to give away or sell your Kindle Fire, you should deregister it first. This removes the Kindle Fire's access to your account and prevents the new owner from using your credit card information.

1. From the Manage Your Kindle page, click Manage Your Devices.

2. Locate the Kindle you want to deregister and click it.

3. Click Deregister.

4. In the Deregister This Device pop-up, click the Deregister button.

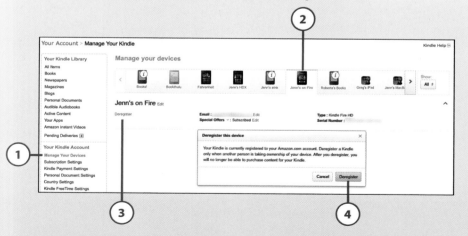

Why Deregister an App?

If your computer, tablet, or mobile phone is lost or stolen, or if you sell or give it away, you should deregister the Kindle app for that device. That way, no purchases can be made against your account without your knowledge.

Renaming Your Kindle Fire

You can change the name of your Kindle device to make it unique and distinguish it from your other Kindles.

1. From Manage Your Devices, click the Kindle whose name you want to change.

2. Click Edit next to the existing name.

3. Enter a new name for your Kindle.

4. Click Save.

Naming Your Kindle Fire

The name of your device appears in the left corner of the status bar. Unless you want to stare at something like "Jennifer's 2nd Kindle" every day, you might want to change it.

Turning Off Special Offers

Your Kindle Fire displays special offers and ads that appear on the screensaver and in the Offers heading of the Navigation bar. You can pay a one-time fee to remove these offers.

1. In Manage Your Devices, locate the device you want to unsubscribe from special offers.

2. Click Edit in the Special Offers column.

3. Click Unsubscribe Now with 1-Click. Your account is charged $15 to unsubscribe a Kindle Fire from these offers. The cost to unsubscribe other Kindle Devices varies.

Why Should I Have to Pay?

Amazon charges advertising fees for special offers, which they claim subsidizes the cost of the Kindle Fire. Thus, if you opt out, their rationale is that they expect you to pay the projected difference in cost. Many people are not disturbed by the placement of the offers, so I advise you to use your Kindle Fire for a while to see whether removing them is worth the additional cost.

Turning Off Whispersync

Whispersync keeps all your devices and Kindle apps synchronized. It synchronizes your reading position, notes, highlights, and more. If you personally use multiple devices or apps when reading a book, keep Whispersync turned on. If multiple people in your home read Kindles registered to the same account, disable Whispersync so that each device can maintain unique page positions, highlights, and notes for a book.

1. From Manage Your Kindle, click Whispersync Device Synchronization.

2. Click Turn Off or Turn On to toggle Whispersync. This change takes effect immediately.

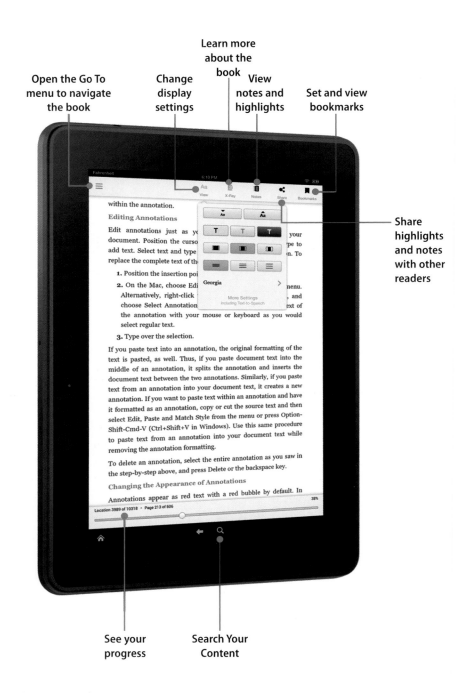

Open the Go To menu to navigate the book

Change display settings

Learn more about the book

View notes and highlights

Set and view bookmarks

Share highlights and notes with other readers

See your progress

Search Your Content

In this chapter you learn about finding content for your Kindle Fire and how to read and interact with that content. You also discover how you can search your Kindle Fire libraries.

Reading on the Kindle Fire

Your Kindle Fire is a great tablet computer, but it's still a Kindle ebook reader at heart. Its size makes it convenient to carry with you so that you can read your books, magazines, newspapers, and other content no matter where you are. When it's inconvenient for you to look at the page, the Kindle Fire's audiobook immersion and text-to-speech features can even read for you.

Finding Content

Amazon's Kindle Store provides access to a huge assortment of reading content for your Kindle Fire. You can find just about any book you want to read for the Kindle. In addition to books, Amazon offers a wide array of newspapers and magazines. Because your Kindle Fire's screen is full color, reading periodicals can provide a similar experience to reading a glossy magazine. Reading has also become an auditory experience as much as a visual one, and your Kindle Fire can play audiobooks. If you have both the ebook and audiobook copies of a title, you can immerse yourself in the reading experience, following along with the professional narration, and keep both books in sync.

Your source of great content doesn't stop with Amazon. You can also check out books from your local library, borrow books from friends and family, and even download books from other online ebook stores and websites, and then transfer them to your Kindle Fire.

Accessing Non-Amazon Books

Many other online bookstores deliver your books using your Kindle's email address and the personal document delivery system. You can read more about setting up a unique Kindle email address in Chapter 3, "Using Amazon's Manage Your Kindle Page," and about personal documents in Chapter 10, "Managing Your Personal Documents and Data."

Buying Books

Amazon's Kindle Store has more than 1 million books available for your Kindle Fire.

1. From the home screen, tap Books.

2. Tap Store.

3. Tap See More to view more titles in a listing.

4. To view books in a particular category, swipe from the left edge of the screen toward the middle, or tap the navigation menu icon to open the Go To menu.

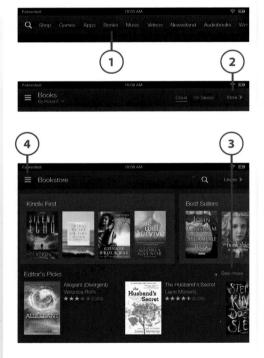

5. Tap Browse Categories. You can also select one of the other Go To menu options to view all the titles in that listing.

6. Tap the category of books you want to view.

7. Tap a book that you want to read on your Kindle Fire.

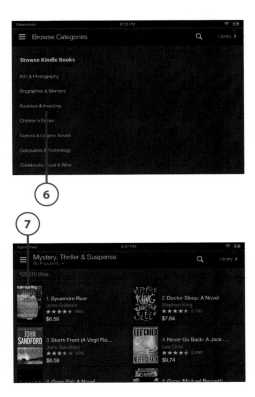

8. If you're trying out a new author or genre, download a free sample first. A free sample is generally the first 10% of a book, sometimes along with the table of contents and other introductory material.

9. Tap Buy to purchase the book and add it to your Kindle library.

Using the Kindle Lending Library

If you are a Prime subscriber, you can borrow one book per month from the thousands of books in Amazon's Kindle Owners' Lending Library. You can keep borrowed books as long as you want, but you can borrow only one book in a calendar month.

Check Out Your Local Library

You can also check out Kindle books from thousands of local libraries. To find out if your local library offers this service, go to www.overdrive.com and enter your ZIP Code.

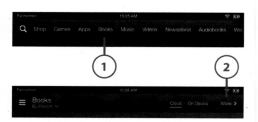

1. From the home screen, tap Books.

2. Tap Store to open the Kindle Store.

3. Locate a book. Books available from the Kindle Lending Library are marked in search results with a Prime badge.

4. Tap Borrow for Free to borrow the book and add it to your library.

Can't Borrow?

If a book is not available for borrowing, the Borrow for Free button isn't visible. If you've already borrowed a book during the past month, the Borrow for Free button is grayed out.

Only on Kindle Devices

You can borrow or read books from the Kindle Lending Library only on a Kindle device; you cannot borrow or read them from your web browser or any other Kindle app.

Completing Your Book Collection with MatchBook

Most people have acquired a library of print books long before they purchased their Kindle Fire device. Amazon has launched a service called MatchBook that allows you to purchase discounted ebook versions of print books you've previously purchased from Amazon.

1. In your web browser (on your computer or the Silk browser on your Kindle Fire), hover over (or tap if you're using the Silk browser on your Kindle Fire) Shop by Department.

2. Hover over or tap Kindle E-Readers.

3. Click Kindle Books.

4. Click Kindle MatchBook.

5. Click Find Your Kindle MatchBook Titles.

6. When the page displays books that match your Amazon print purchases, tap Get Kindle Edition to purchase a book at the discounted Kindle MatchBook price.

7. Complete your purchase by selecting the device to which you want the ebook delivered, and then click Buy Now with 1-Click.

Amazon MatchBook Is Limited

Amazon launched the MatchBook service in October 2013, so the titles available are currently limited. Although this service is expected to grow, it is unlikely that you can replace your entire print library with discounted ebook versions.

It's Not All Good

Purchasing Print Editions of Ebooks

MatchBook does not work in both directions. If you purchase an ebook through Amazon, you cannot get a discount on the print edition. If you know you'll want a book in both editions, purchase the print edition first in hopes that the title is available in MatchBook.

Lending Books to Friends and Family

You can loan some books to friends or family. Your friend or family member isn't required to have a Kindle device to read the book you lend. Loaned books can be read on a computer or other device with the free Kindle application.

1. Open your web browser and go to www.amazon.com/manageyourkindle.

2. Hover your mouse pointer over the Actions drop-down next to the title you want to lend.

3. Click Loan This Title.

4. Enter your friend or family member's information and a personal message.

5. Click Send Now.

What Happens Next?

When you lend a book, the recipient of the book receives an email with a link to accept the request. That person needs an Amazon account to accept and access the book. If they do not already have a Kindle device or app, they are prompted to download the appropriate Kindle app for their computer or device.

Books are loaned for 14 days, and you are not able to read the book while it is loaned out to someone. You can see the status of the loan on the Manage Your Kindle page.

It's Not All Good

Why Can't I Lend My Book?

The publisher of a book decides whether an ebook can be loaned to others. If a publisher hasn't granted that right, the option to lend the book is not available.

You can determine whether a book can be loaned to others by reviewing the Product Details for the book on Amazon's website. If the book can be loaned, it displays Lending: Enabled. Unfortunately, this information is not available from the Kindle Store listings on the Kindle Fire.

Subscribing to Periodicals

The Kindle Store offers a wide array of newspapers and magazines, including some that are optimized with multimedia content specifically for the Kindle Fire.

1. From the home screen, tap Newsstand to open the Newsstand.

2. Tap Store to open the Kindle Newsstand.

3. Choose a magazine or newspaper you want to read.

4. Tap Subscribe Now to download the latest edition to your Kindle Fire or tap Buy Issue to buy and download only the current issue.

Trial Subscriptions

Most periodicals provide a trial subscription, for which you are not charged. Unless you cancel your subscription within the trial period, you are charged the day after the trial concludes and then monthly thereafter.

Organizing Your Books

The Kindle has always been a great device for reading. Instead of carrying around a pile of books, you can put everything you want to read on your Kindle. Look up definitions with the integrated dictionary or search the Web when you want to read more about something you encounter in a book. You can even increase the size of a book's text to make it easier to read.

Browsing Your Library

After you buy or borrow a book or download a sample from the Kindle Store, it appears in the Books content library and in the Carousel on the home screen. You can view books on your device and in the cloud using the Books library.

1. From the home screen, tap Books to access your Books library.

2. Tap On Device to see content that has been downloaded to your Kindle Fire, or tap Cloud to see content that is in your online library.

3. Tap By Author, By Recent, or By Title to change the order in which your books are sorted.

Downloading a Book to Your Device

Before you can read a book, you must download it to your Kindle Fire. If you purchase a book from the Kindle Store on your device, it is automatically downloaded onto the Kindle Fire. If you purchased the book using the Amazon website, it is available from any device linked to your account via the Amazon Cloud.

1. From the Books library, tap Cloud to see the books in your online library.

2. Scroll to the book you want to download to your device.

3. Tap the book to download it to your device.

Cloud and Device

When you are in Cloud view, you see books that are also on your device. That's because, even after you download a book to your device, it's still in the cloud so that you can download it to other Kindles or apps.

Books that you have downloaded to your device have a check mark in the lower-right corner.

It's Not All Good

Sharing Your Amazon Account

Any books you purchase from Amazon are automatically stored in the Amazon Cloud. If you share your Amazon account with other members of your family, particularly your children, be aware that they can easily download any of your purchases onto their own Kindle devices or Kindle app. If you want to limit your child's access to mature reading material, your only recourse on the Kindle Fire is to block them from the Books content library entirely or set up a Kindle FreeTime profile for them. There is no way to limit access to books (or videos and music) based on rating or content.

Removing a Book from Your Device

You can remove downloaded books from your Kindle Fire to free up memory on the device. This is not the same as deleting a book from your Amazon account, as described in Chapter 3. Your books are still available in the cloud, so you can download them again at any time.

1. From the Books library, tap On Device to see the books on your device.

2. Tap and hold the book that you want to remove from your device.

3. Tap Remove from Device.

Creating a Collection

If you're a voracious reader, the biggest challenge of reading on your Kindle Fire is keeping your book collection organized. Cloud Collections allow you to create custom collections of books. You can create a category for Classics, for example, and add all your classic works to that collection.

1. From within Books, tap the menu icon or swipe from the left edge of the screen to the center to open the navigational menu.

2. Tap Collections.

3. Tap the Add icon.

4. Enter a name for the collection.

5. Tap Add.

6. Tap the box to the right of titles to add books to the new collection.

7. Scroll down to view more books.

8. Tap Add.

It's Not All Good

Cloud Collections Are Somewhat Rudimentary

Although collections are a huge step forward for organizing books on your Kindle Fire, the implementation of this feature still has its flaws. If you rename a collection, it no longer appears in proper alphabetical order. You cannot change the sort order of collections to keep the most recently used collection at the top of the screen. You also can't change the order in which books appear within a collection; new books are appended to the end of the collection rather than placed at the top, so you need to scroll down within the collection to find your newest additions.

Editing a Collection

You can add one or more books to a collection from within the Collections screen.

1. In Collections, tap a collection.

2. Tap Add.

3. Tap the checkmarks to the right of the titles of books you want to add to the collection, scrolling down to view additional titles as needed.

4. Tap Add.

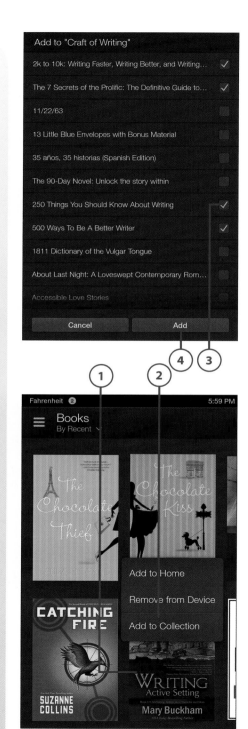

Adding a Book to a Collection

You can also add books to one or more collections by selecting the book from the Books screen.

1. In Books, tap and hold the book you want to add to a collection.

2. Tap Add to Collection.

3. Tap the collection to which you want to add the book. You can add a book to more than one collection.

4. Tap Add.

Add to Collection

⊕ New Collection

Classics

Craft of Writing ✓

Fantasy

Fiction

Gaiman

General Fiction

Harlequin and Other Series

Harry Potter

Here and Now

Historical

Cancel   Add

Removing a Book from a Collection

You can remove books from a collection without removing them from your device or the Cloud.

1. From the Collections screen, tap a collection.

2. Tap and hold a book you want to remove from the collection.

3. When the Remove button appears, you can tap additional books in the collection to mark them for removal.

4. Tap Remove to remove the books from the collection. Tap Done to escape the Removal screen without removing any books.

Reading on Your Kindle

The Kindle Fire is a great device for reading. Its backlit screen allows you to easily read in low-light conditions without a reading light. Your book always opens to the page you last read, so you don't have to worry about dog-earing pages or losing your place. If you don't know the meaning of a word, you can look up the definition on the spot.

My Book Doesn't Open on Page One

Kindle books open at the beginning of the book, but the beginning isn't necessarily page one. The publisher of an ebook can choose any page as the beginning of a book. Ebooks frequently open at a point after the front matter—the cover, table of contents, foreword, and dedication. You can use the Go To button to access this material.

Reading a Book

Books appear in your Books library and on the home screen Carousel. Reading a book on the Kindle Fire is as simple as tapping your finger.

1. From the Books library or the Carousel, tap a book to open it for reading.

2. Tap the right side of a page or swipe from right to left to move forward one page.

3. Tap the left side of a page or swipe from left to right to move back one page.

4. See an estimate of how much time it should take you to finish the current chapter or book.

Changing the Time to Read Display

As you read, your Kindle Fire calculates your reading speed and provides estimates of how much time it should take you to finish reading the current chapter or book. This information is stored only on your Kindle Fire, so if you are reading on multiple devices or apps, this estimate will not be accurate.

To change the Time to Read display, tap on it in the lower-left corner of the screen. The setting toggles to display time to read the chapter, time to read the book, the current page, the current location, and blank.

LES MISÉRABLES (ENGLISH LANGUAGE)

BOOK FIRST—A JUST MAN

CHAPTER I—M. MYRIEL

In 1815, M. Charles-Francois-Bienvenu Myriel was Bishop of D—— He was an old man of about seventy-five years of age; he had occupied the see of D—— since 1806.

Although this detail has no connection whatever with the real substance of what we are about to relate, it will not be superfluous, if merely for the sake of exactness in all points, to mention here the various rumors and remarks which had been in circulation about him from the very moment when he arrived in the diocese. True or false, that which is said of men often occupies as important a place in their lives, and above all in their destinies, as that which they do. M. Myriel was the son of a councillor of the Parliament of Aix; hence he belonged to the nobility of the bar. It was said that his father, destining him to be the heir of his own post, had married him at a very early age, eighteen or twenty, in accordance with a custom which is rather widely prevalent in parliamentary families. In spite of this marriage, however, it was said that Charles Myriel created a great deal of talk. He was well formed, though rather short in stature, elegant, graceful, intelligent; the whole of the first portion of his life had been devoted to the world and to gallantry.

Navigating a Book

You can quickly access any page in a book, including the front matter.

1. Tap the center of the page.

2. Swipe the Location slider to move forward or backward within the book.

3. Tap the navigation menu button or swipe from the left edge of the screen toward the center to open the Go To menu.

4. Tap Go to Page or Location to go to a specific location or page number.

5. Tap Sync to Furthest Page Read to return to the furthest page you've read in the book. If you have Whispersync turned on, as explained in Chapter 3, this button syncs to the furthest page you've read on any of your Kindle devices or apps.

6. Tap an item in the Table of Contents to go directly to that chapter or front matter element.

7. Tap Back to Books Library to return to the content library.

8. Tap the cover image to go to the Kindle Store listing for the book.

9. Tap the navigation menu button or swipe from the right edge of the Go To menu to the left edge of the screen to return to the page you were reading.

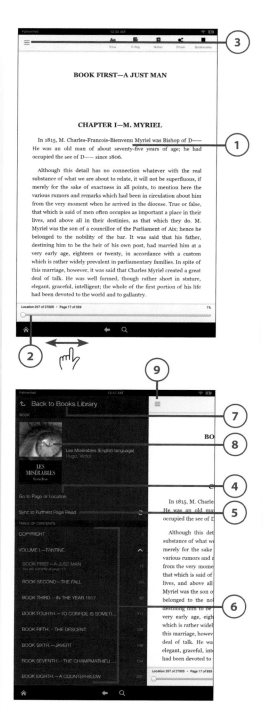

Where Are the Page Numbers?

Some ebooks use location numbers; others use traditional page numbers. Because text can be repaginated based on the text size you use, location numbers provide a better sense of where you are in the book. Traditional page numbers, when available, make it easier to refer to a particular page when discussing a book with friends or book clubs, however.

Changing Font Styles

You can change the size of fonts, line spacing, page margins, and colors when reading Kindle content.

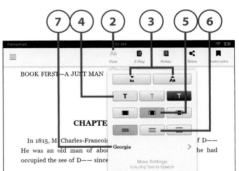

1. Tap the center of a page while you're reading.

2. Tap the View icon.

3. Tap the Font Size option to make the text larger or smaller. You can tap the appropriate button multiple times to get the size you want.

4. Tap a Color Mode to change the color of the page background and text.

5. Tap a Margins option to change the way the page is spread across the display.

6. Tap a Line Spacing option to change the amount of space between lines.

7. Tap the Font option to select a different typeface.

8. Choose a typeface from the options available.

Font Size and Typeface Are Not Just in Books

You can change font size and typeface settings in books, newspapers, personal documents, and magazines.

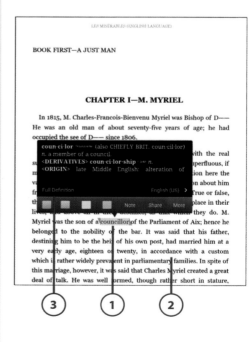

Looking Up Definitions

Your Kindle Fire comes with *The New Oxford American Dictionary* so that you can look up definitions of words while you're reading. Definitions are available from books, magazines, newspapers, and your personal documents.

1. Tap and hold the word you want to look up. A definition of the word displays.

2. Tap your book page to dismiss the pop-up definition.

3. Tap Full Definition to open the dictionary and see a more detailed definition.

4. To return to your book after viewing a full definition, tap the center of the screen and then tap the Back icon.

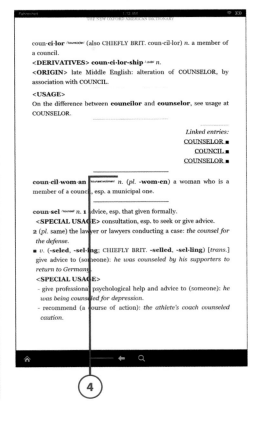

Working with Notes and Highlights
================================

Just as when marking up a physical book, notes and highlights are a convenient way of annotating important passages. Notes are available in books and in personal documents that are in Mobi format. (Kindle files in Mobi format have either a .mobi or a .prc file extension.) Highlights are available in books and personal documents (that are in Mobi format), but you cannot highlight periodicals.

Notes enable you to visually locate a passage, along with personal comments that you attach to that passage. Highlights allow you to visually locate a passage again, but without personal comments.

Adding a Note

You can add a note to any book, whether you own the book or not (although you cannot add notes to samples of books). Notes that you add to a book are synchronized across all your Kindle devices and Kindle apps.

1. In an open book, tap and hold to begin selecting a passage to which you want to attach a note.

2. If necessary, tap and drag on the left and right of a selection to select more or fewer words.

3. Tap Note.

4. Enter the text for your note using the Kindle keyboard.

5. Tap Save to save the note.

6. To cancel a note, tap away from the Note pop-up.

Viewing an Individual Note

Notes appear as highlighted text with a blue note icon. You can view an individual note by tapping it.

1. Tap the blue note icon that marks your note.

2. After reviewing your note, tap Close.

Again he wrote: "Do not inquire the name of him who asks a shelter of you. The very man who is embarrassed by his name is the one who needs shelter."

1

house so little guarded. The Bishop touched his shoulder,

Page 32 - Note

So what should you call him?

Close   Delete   Edit

2

Editing a Note

You can easily edit notes, and any edits you make are synchronized across all your Kindle devices.

1. Tap the blue note icon that marks your note.

2. Tap Edit.

3. Enter the new text for your note.

4. Tap Save to commit your changes.

Again he wrote: "Do not inquire the name of him who asks a shelter of you. The very man who is embarrassed by his name is the one who needs shelter."

1

house so little guarded. The Bishop touched his shoulder,

Page 32 - Note

So what should you call him?

Close   Delete   Edit

3   **2** **4**

the bravery of a colonel of dragoons,—only," he added, "ours must be

So what should you call him? Monsieur Smith?   Save

| 1 | 2 | 3 | 4 | 5 | 6 | 7 | 8 | 9 | 0 |

@ $ _ ( ) : ; ' "

~\< - ! # = / + ?

ABC

Deleting a Note

When you delete a note, you delete it across all your Kindle devices.

1. Tap the blue note icon that marks your note.

2. Tap Delete.

3. Tap Delete to confirm.

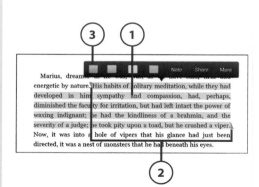

Adding a Highlight

As with the highlights in a physical book, a highlighted passage in a Kindle Fire book appears as yellow highlighted words.

1. Tap and hold to begin selecting a passage you want to highlight.

2. If necessary, tap and drag on the left and right of a selection to select more or fewer words.

3. Tap a highlight color.

Viewing All Notes and Highlights

You can view a list of all your notes, highlights, and bookmarks for a particular book.

1. Tap the center of a page to access the Options bar.

2. Tap Notes to open the My Notes & Marks screen.

3. Tap a note or mark to go to that location in the book.

4. To exit the My Notes & Marks screen without selecting a note or highlight, tap the X icon.

Deleting a Highlight

Unlike highlights in a physical book, you can delete a highlight in a Kindle book. The steps described here are also an alternative way to delete notes.

1. Tap the center of a page to access the Options bar.

2. Tap Notes to open the My Notes & Marks screen.

3. Tap and hold the highlight (or note) you want to delete.

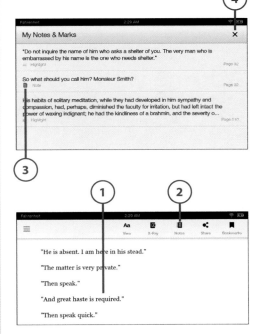

4. Tap Delete.

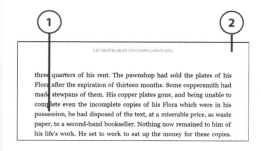

4

Location 14273 - Highlight

View

Delete

Change highlight color to pink

Change highlight color to blue

Change highlight color to orange

No Confirmation for Deleting Highlights

When you delete a highlight, you aren't asked whether you really want to delete it. If you think about it, this isn't a big deal because you can just highlight a passage again if you delete it in error.

Working with Bookmarks

When you're reading a physical book, a bookmark enables you to mark your place so that you can easily return to it. The Kindle Fire marks your place automatically, but you still might want to add bookmarks on important pages so that you can easily locate them later. Think of these bookmarks as a dog-eared page. In fact, you can bookmark as many pages as you want in a book.

Bookmarks are available in books and in personal documents that are in Mobi format.

Adding a Bookmark

Adding a bookmark is easy. Bookmarks that you add are synchronized across all your Kindle devices and applications.

1   **2**

LES MISÉRABLES (ENGLISH LANGUAGE)

three quarters of his rent. The pawnshop had sold the plates of his Flora after the expiration of thirteen months. Some coppersmith had made stewpans of them. His copper plates gone, and being unable to complete even the incomplete copies of his Flora which were in his possession, he had disposed of the text, at a miserable price, as waste paper, to a second-hand bookseller. Nothing now remained to him of his life's work. He set to work to eat up the money for these copies.

1. Move to the page where you want to add your bookmark.

2. Tap the upper-right corner of the page to add a bookmark.

Removing a Bookmark

When you remove a bookmark, you remove it from all Kindle devices and applications.

1. Move to the page that is bookmarked.

2. Tap the blue bookmark icon to remove the bookmark.

Easy Bookmark Removal

Bookmarks can also be deleted from the My Notes & Marks screen. Tap and hold the bookmark you want to remove and tap Delete.

Moving to a Bookmark

You can easily move to a page that you've bookmarked using the My Notes & Marks screen.

1. Tap the center of a page while reading your book.

2. Tap Bookmarks in the Options bar.

3. Tap a bookmark to move directly to the bookmarked page.

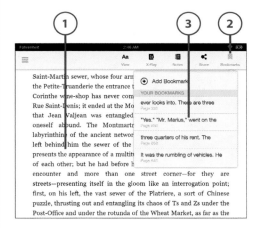

Reading Magazines and Newspapers

The Kindle Fire is a wonderful way to read magazines and newspapers. The full-color screen and the touch interface make the experience of reading periodicals similar to that of reading a physical magazine.

Reading Magazines

Most of the magazines, and some of the newspapers, that are available in the Kindle Store offer dynamic content that represents the look of the actual printed magazine while also offering easy navigation. This is called *page-view*.

1. From the home screen, tap Newsstand.

2. Tap Cloud to view the magazines and newspapers to which you have subscribed.

3. Tap a magazine to download the current issue to your device. If there is more than one issue of a magazine available, the number of issues appears in the lower-left corner.

4. Tap On Device to view magazines and newspapers downloaded to your device.

5. Tap a magazine to open it. If there are multiple issues of a magazine on your device, tap the issue you want to read.

6. Tap the center of a page to display the Options bar.

7. Tap Browse to view the table of contents for the magazine.

8. Swipe across the thumbnails to quickly move through the pages.

9. Tap a page thumbnail to move to that page.

10. Swipe up and down to navigate within an article. Swipe left or right to move forward or back to another article in the magazine.

11. Tap the menu icon or swipe from the left edge of the screen toward the center to view the Go To menu.

12. Tap an article to move directly to it.

Every Magazine Is Different

Many magazines are distributed via their own app, so you may discover that they have different features and navigational elements. Some magazines allow you to zoom in on pieces of content. The display of the table of contents may vary when you tap the Browse icon. Some magazines even include additional content not available in the print edition.

Reading Newspapers

Newspapers and magazines that aren't page-view enabled display in text view.

1. From the Newsstand, tap a newspaper or magazine that is not page-view enabled.

2. Tap the center of a page to show the Progress and Options bars.

3. Tap the arrows on the Progress bar to move forward and backward through articles.

4. Tap the View icon to change text size, typeface, and color options.

5. Swipe left to move forward one page, or swipe right to move back one page. You can also tap the right or left edges of a page to move forward or backward.

6. Tap the menu icon or swipe from the left edge of the screen toward the center to open the Go To menu, which displays a list of articles and sections.

7. Tap an article to go to that article.

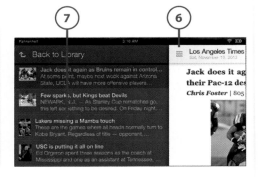

Listening to Audiobooks

Sometimes you want to read a good book, but perhaps you're driving or cooking and you don't have hands or eyes free to read it yourself. Audiobooks are audio editions of books, many of them narrated by celebrities or professional readers.

Not only can your Kindle Fire play audiobooks, but it can sync a bookmark across text and audio versions of the same book using Whispersync for Voice. You can also use Immersion Reading to follow along in the text while listening to the audiobook version.

Downloading Audiobooks

Audiobooks are sold in the Amazon Store through Audible. The first time you make an audiobook purchase, you're prompted to try a new Audible membership. If you already have an Audible account, you're asked to verify it.

1. Tap Audiobooks from the Navigation bar.

2. Tap Store.

3. Select an audiobook.

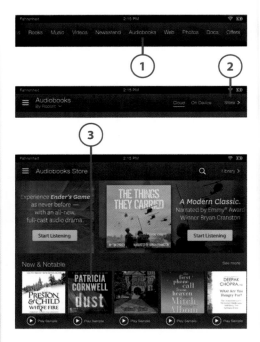

4. Play a sample if you want to hear the reader's voice before purchasing.

5. If this is your first Audible purchase, you receive an option to sign up for an Audible membership and download two free audiobooks. These appear as credits when you select an audiobook.

6. If you already have an Audible membership, tap the Buy button to purchase the audiobook.

7. Tap Listen Now if you want to start listening to your audiobook immediately. If you have both the ebook and the audiobook of a title, this button says Read & Listen Now.

Listening to Audiobooks

Audiobooks are stored in the Amazon Cloud, available for download onto your device. Find your audiobooks in the Audiobooks library. Audiobooks are almost impossible to complete in one sitting, but don't worry about losing your place. Your Kindle Fire automatically syncs your audiobooks so you can start up again where you left off.

1. From the Audiobooks content library, tap an audiobook to play. If the audiobook has not yet been downloaded to your Kindle Fire, you must download it before you play it.

2. The audiobook automatically begins to play. Press Pause to temporarily stop the audio. Press Play to restart the audio.

3. Tap the Rewind 30 Seconds button to repeat the last 30 seconds of audio.

4. Tap the Bookmark icon to add a bookmark to a point in the audio. Tap and hold to add a note.

5. Swipe the location bar to play in a different location within the current chapter.

6. Tap the Narration Timer icon to change the speed at which the audio plays.

7. Tap the desired reading speed.

8. Tap the Sleep Timer icon to automatically play the audio for a specific amount of time before automatically shutting off.

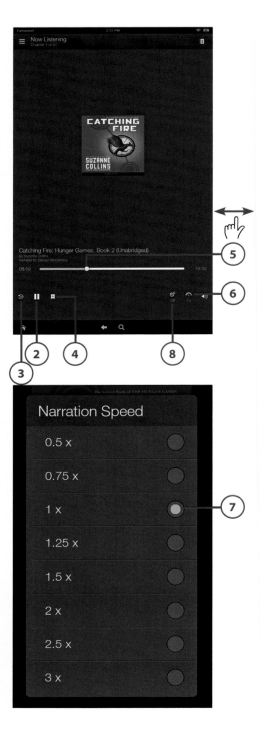

9. Tap the amount of time for the sleep timer. Tap End of Chapter for the audio to play until the end of the chapter, however long that lasts, before shutting off.

10. Tap the navigation menu icon or swipe from the left edge of the screen toward the center to open the Go To menu.

11. Tap a chapter to begin playing that chapter.

Viewing Bookmarks in Audiobooks

If you want to access bookmarks you set in an audiobook, tap the Bookmarks icon in the top-right corner of the screen when the Options bar is displayed.

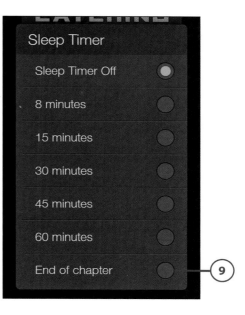

Immersion Reading

If you own both the ebook and audiobook versions of a book, you can use Immersion Reading to read along with the professional narrator.

1. Tap Books in the Navigation bar.

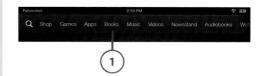

2. Tap the book you want to read and hear.

3. Tap the middle of the screen.

4. Tap Play to read with professional narration.

5. The gray highlights show the text the narrator is reading so you can follow along.

6. Tap Pause to pause the narration.

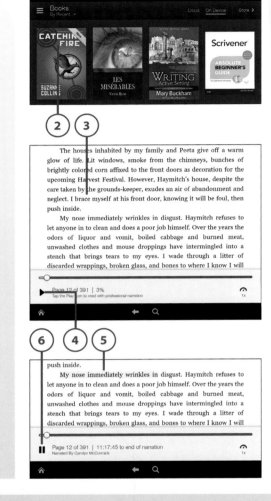

My Book Won't Sync

Immersion Reading is not without its flaws. Although it works well in most circumstances, it occasionally struggles to sync the ebook and audiobook, and you might have to tap the Play button several times to get it to work properly.

GETTING THE MOST OUT OF IMMERSION READING

Studies have shown that bimodal learning improves retention. If you're reading a book for academic purposes, such as Shakespeare, using Immersion Reading stimulates both your visual and your auditory senses, thereby helping you remember it later.

Using Text-to-Speech

Your Kindle Fire can read some books and periodicals even if you do not own the audiobook. Text-to-Speech reads in a very mechanical female voice, unlike the professional narration of audiobooks.

1. In a book, tap the middle of a page.

2. Tap View.

3. Tap More Settings.

4. Tap the On button for Text-to-Speech.

5. Tap the Back button to return to the book.

6. Tap the center of the page.

7. Tap Play to listen to Text-to-Speech. You can pause the narration with the same button.

When Text-to-Speech Is Not Available

The publisher of a book determines whether the Text-to-Speech feature is available for that title.

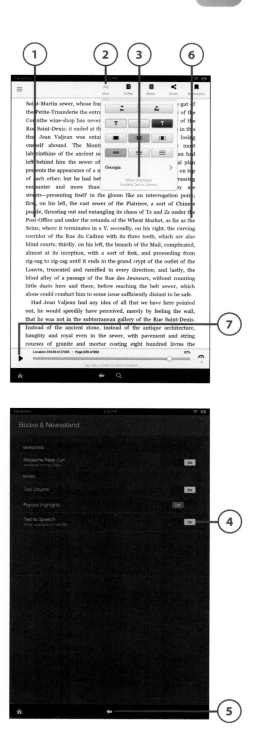

Searching Content and Accessing Reference Materials

Your Kindle Fire provides several ways for you to get more information about your books. The device automatically maintains a searchable index of all the content in your libraries. You can also search in Wikipedia or Google. If you want to learn more about the book you're reading, X-Ray offers character breakdowns and other features.

Using X-Ray for Books

X-Ray shows you all the passages that refer to specific characters or terms. If you're reading a textbook, X-Ray can even act as a dynamic index.

1. Tap the middle of a page in the book you want to x-ray.

2. Tap X-Ray.

3. Examine the current page or chapter or the entire book.

4. Examine all the entries in the book or tap People or Terms to limit the material.

5. Tap an entry to see a list of all references for that character or term.

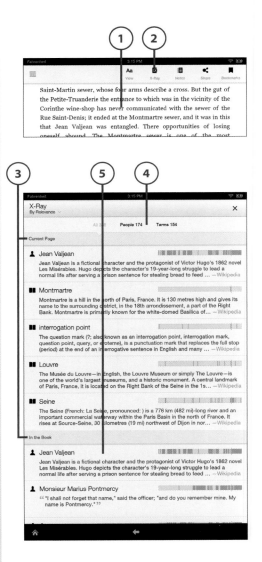

6. Tap an entry to go to the source page for a reference.

Missing X-Rays

As with text-to-speech and certain other features, the availability of X-Ray is up to the publisher.

Searching the Current Item

You can search for one or more words in an item that you're reading.

1. While reading the item you want to search, tap the middle of a page.

2. Tap the Search icon.

3. Enter your search words in the Search box.

4. Tap Go.

5. Wait for the progress bar while the search completes.

6. Scroll to locate a specific search result.

7. Tap to move to the search result in the text.

Searching Wikipedia or Bing from Books

You can search the Web or Wikipedia for words that you select in books. If you select more than two words, these options aren't available.

1. Select one or two words you want to search for.

2. Tap More.

3. Tap Search the Web to search for the selected word(s) in your selected search engine in the Silk browser.

4. Tap Search Wikipedia to search for the selected word(s) in Wikipedia.

5. When you've finished reading the search results, tap the Back button to go back to your book.

Selecting a Search Engine

Your Kindle Fire uses Microsoft Bing as the default search engine. I explain how to change this in Chapter 12, "Browsing the Web with Silk."

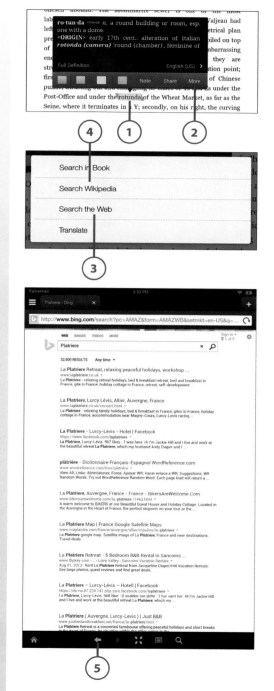

Browse music

View your cloud
and device music

Stream your music
over the Internet

In this chapter, you learn how to access and listen to music on your Kindle Fire. Topics include the following:

- → Browsing and downloading your music
- → Playing music
- → Managing playlists

Listening to Music on the Kindle Fire

The Kindle Fire is arguably the best way to play music that you have stored on Amazon's Cloud Player. Because it has a limited amount of user-accessible memory, you likely can't carry all your music on it when you're offline, but you can make playlists and download some of your music to enjoy when you're away from a Wi-Fi connection.

In addition to playing music, you can browse Amazon's extensive library of MP3s to add to your music collection.

Browsing and Downloading Your Music

Your Kindle Fire integrates directly into your Cloud Drive and provides a first-class interface into browsing and listening to your music. As soon as you start your Kindle Fire for the first time (after you've signed in to your Amazon account on the device), it begins indexing the music on your Cloud Drive.

This chapter deals primarily with music in the cloud because that's likely the way you'll listen to music on your Kindle Fire. However, all the information presented also applies to interacting with music stored on your device.

Add Music to Your Cloud Drive

If you haven't added any music to your Cloud Drive, see Chapter 2, "Accessing Amazon's Cloud Services," for information on how to do that.

Browsing Music

Your Kindle Fire can provide you with a list of all artists in your music collection, in alphabetical order.

1. From the home screen, tap Music.

2. Tap Cloud to view your Cloud Drive.

3. Tap the navigation menu icon or swipe from the left edge of the screen toward the center to open the Go To menu.

4. Tap Artists, Albums, Songs, or Genres to display the music in your collection grouped by your selection.

5. Scroll up and down to view music.

6. Tap an artist, album, or genre to see a list of music in your collection within that selection.

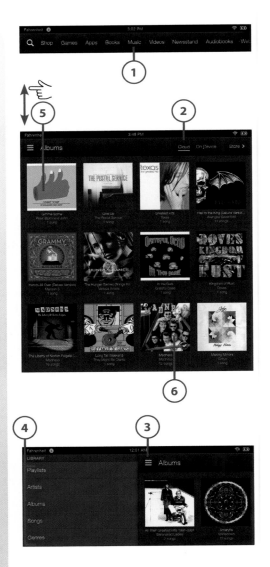

7. To listen to this music even with-
    out an active Internet connection,
    tap Download All. This downloads
    all the songs included in your
    selection to your device.

8. Tap Explore Artist to access more
    music by that artist in the Amazon
    Music Store. You can also tap
    Store in the upper-right corner to
    access the Amazon Music Store
    home page.

9. Tap the album cover to learn
    more about an album in the
    Amazon Music Store.

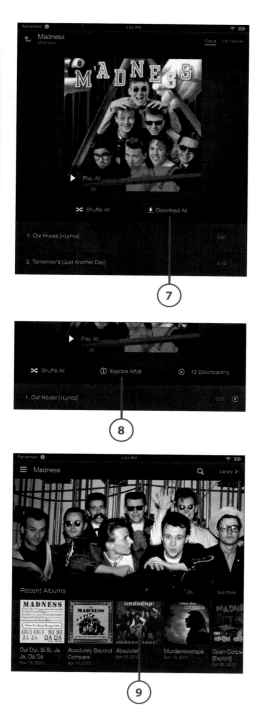

10. Tap the Play button to hear a sample of a song.

11. Tap Sample All to hear samples of the entire album.

12. Tap the purchase price to purchase the song.

13. Tap Buy Album to purchase the entire album.

ALBUM ONLY

Some songs are listed as Album Only and cannot be purchased individually. This restriction most often appears on extra content, such as digital booklets, that accompany some albums. It might also appear on compilation albums in which particular songs are sold as part of the compilation and not individually. If you want to access this content, you must purchase the complete album.

>>>Go Further

Scrolling Through Your Music

Having a large number of artists, albums, or songs in your music collection is not uncommon. To more quickly find an item, scroll to items that begin with a particular letter of the alphabet. If you are viewing your collection by Album, Artist, or Genre, your music appears in Grid view by default, so you need to first switch to List view. If you are viewing your collection by Song, it automatically appears in List view, in which case you can skip step 1 below.

1. In the Music content library, tap the menu icon in the Options bar.

2. From the list of music items, swipe to begin scrolling.

3. As soon as the scroll handle appears, immediately tap and hold it.

4. Drag the scroll handle up and down to quickly browse by letter.

5. Release the scroll handle when the desired letter appears on the screen to jump to items that begin with that letter.

Monitoring Downloads from an Album

As your music tracks download, you can monitor their progress and cancel the download, if necessary.

1. Locate an artist, album, or song you want to download.

2. Tap Download All.

3. Tap the X if you want to cancel the download for a particular song.

Searching Your Music Collection

Your Kindle Fire can search both music that's on your device and music in the cloud. You can search for playlists, artists, albums, or songs.

1. In the Music app, tap the Search icon.

2. Enter your search term in the Search box. Results appear as you type.

3. Tap the item you seek. The search results list items from both the cloud and the device.

Sorting Through Search Results

If you are in the Music app when you begin your search, the first set of search results is from your Music library. These results are followed by items matching your search term from other Kindle Fire content libraries.

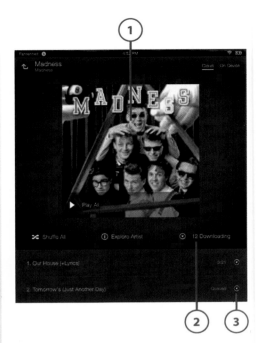

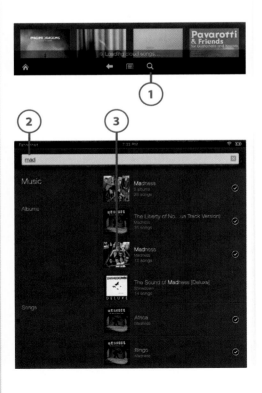

Playing Music

Your Kindle Fire can play music you've downloaded to the device or stream music directly from your Cloud Drive. When you stream music, you need an Internet connection. If you're going to be in an area where you cannot connect to the Internet, plan ahead by downloading music so that it will be available no matter where you go.

Listening to Music

You can play music either through the speakers built into the Kindle Fire or through headphones or an external speaker system. After you begin playing music, you can do other tasks on your Kindle Fire, such as read a book or send an email, while the music continues playing.

1. Locate and tap the song you want to hear. This brings up the Now Playing screen.

2. Tap or drag the location slider to move to a particular point in the song. As you drag it, an indicator displays your position in the song.

3. Tap Previous to move to the beginning of the song. Double-tap to move to the previous song.

4. Tap Next to move to the next song.

5. Tap Pause to pause the music.

6. Tap Repeat to repeat all the songs in the Now Playing queue. Tap Repeat again to repeat only the currently playing song.

7. Tap Shuffle to randomly play the songs in the Now Playing queue. Tap it again to turn off shuffle playback.

8. Tap Volume to open the volume slider; then drag the slider up or down to adjust the volume.

Accessing More Options

While viewing the Now Playing screen, tap and hold the album art for a menu of other ways you can interact with your music, including adding the song to a playlist, shopping for more music by the artist, and download-ing the song (if you're currently streaming it) to your device.

Viewing Song Lyrics

You can view the lyrics for some songs using the X-Ray Lyrics feature. This feature is not available for all songs, but you can easily determine which songs have it available, because they appear with [+Lyrics] appended to the song title.

1. Tap a song with the [+Lyrics] designation.

2. As the song plays, the lyrics appear above the music controls.

3. Tap a line in the lyrics to play the song from that line.

4. In portrait mode, to close the lyrics while continuing to play the song, tap the slider above the lyrics and drag down to the music controls.

Note

To improve the display of song lyrics, turn your Kindle Fire to landscape mode. The lyrics appear in a larger font to the right of the music art.

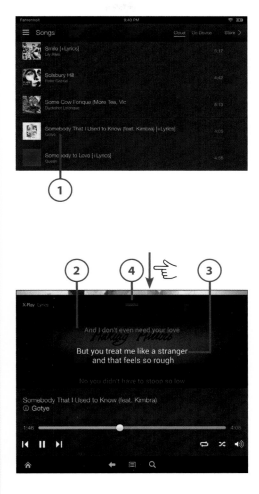

Accessing Music Controls

You don't have to remain in the Music app while playing music. You can access playback controls or see the title and artist of the song that's currently playing while in any other app.

1. Swipe down from the status bar. If you're reading a book or periodical, tap the middle of the page first to display the status bar.

2. Tap the Pause button to pause the music.

3. Tap the Previous button to move to the previous song.

4. Tap the Next button to move to the next song.

5. Tap the name of the song to bring up the Now Playing screen.

6. Swipe up from the bottom of the screen to return to what you were doing.

Managing Playlists

Playlists enable you to create a list of tracks that you want to play. You can create playlists on your device or in the cloud. If you create a playlist in the cloud, that playlist can be accessed both from your computer and from another device that can access your Cloud Player.

You create playlists on your device by first tapping the Device tab. If you tap the Cloud tab first, your playlist is created on your Cloud Player. Playlists that you create on your device can contain only songs that are downloaded to your device. Playlists that you create on your Cloud Player can contain any of your music that is on your Cloud Player.

Creating a Playlist

To create a playlist, decide where you want to create it (on the device or in the cloud) and then go to your Music library.

1. From your Music library, tap the navigation menu icon or drag from the left edge of the screen toward the center to open the Go To menu.

2. Tap Playlists.

3. Tap Cloud to create a playlist from tracks in your Cloud Player, or tap On Device to create a playlist from tracks on your device.

4. Tap the plus sign (+) to create a new playlist.

5. Enter a name for your playlist.

6. Tap Save.

7. Add songs to your playlist by tapping the + sign next to the song.

8. Tap the Search Your Music field and enter a song, album, or artist name to search for tracks.

9. Tap Done when you're finished adding songs.

Cannot Move Device Playlist to the Cloud

When you create a playlist on your device, that playlist can contain only songs that are on your device. You cannot move a playlist created on your device to the cloud, but you can move a playlist created in the cloud to your device.

Editing a Playlist

After you've created a playlist and added your initial songs, you can add or remove songs, or adjust the order in which they play, by editing the playlist.

1. From the Playlists screen, tap your playlist.

2. Tap Edit.

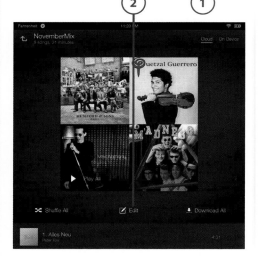

3. Tap Rename to rename the play-
    list, and then enter a new name.

4. Tap the minus sign (–)to remove a
    song from the playlist.

5. Tap and hold the icon at the left
    edge of a song, and drag to a new
    position in the playlist to reorder
    songs.

6. Tap the Add Songs button to add
    new songs using the same inter-
    face you used when creating the
    playlist.

7. Tap Done to save your changes.

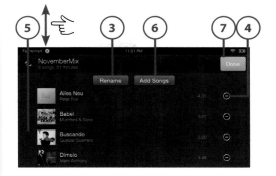

Adding Artists or Albums to a Playlist

You can add songs to a playlist
when you edit the playlist, as I just
explained, or whenever you come
across music you want to add.
Instead of adding songs one track at
a time, you can also add all songs by
an artist or in a particular album.

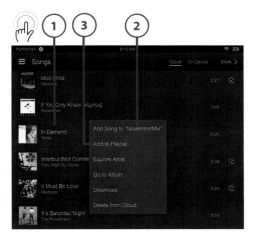

1. Tap and hold the song, artist, or
    album that you want to add to a
    playlist.

2. If you want to add the music to
    the most recent playlist, tap Add
    Song to (the name of the playlist).

3. If you want to add the music to
    a different playlist, tap Add to
    Playlist.

4. Tap the playlist to which you want
    to add the music. Alternatively,
    tap Create New Playlist to create a
    new playlist.

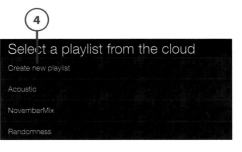

5. If creating a new playlist, give it a name.

6. Tap Save to save the new playlist. You can then edit the new playlist to add more songs to it, as described previously.

Playing a Playlist

Playlists that are on your device can be played only on your Kindle Fire. When you create playlists in the cloud, you can play them on your Kindle Fire or other devices that can access your Cloud Player.

1. From your Music library, tap the menu icon or drag from the left edge of the screen toward the center to open the navigation menu.

2. Tap Playlists.

3. Tap Cloud to see playlists on your Cloud Drive, or tap On Device to see playlists on your Kindle Fire.

4. Tap the playlist you want to play.

5. Tap a song in the playlist to start playing from that song onward.

6. Tap Shuffle All to play the songs in random order.

Downloading a Playlist

You can't play playlists that you create in your Cloud Drive unless you have an active Internet connection. If you want to play the playlist when you aren't connected, you first need to download the playlist to your device.

1. From the Playlists screen, tap Cloud.

2. Tap the playlist that you want to download.

3. Tap the Download All button to download the playlist to your device.

Downloaded Playlist

Downloaded playlists appear on the Device tab in the Playlists screen. Both the playlist and all songs in the playlist are downloaded.

It's Not All Good

The Same Playlist, but Different

When you download a playlist from the cloud to your device, it is initially an identical match. In essence, however, you have created two playlists. If you edit one playlist, your changes are not reflected in the other playlist. I recommend changing the name of your playlist after downloading it so you don't confuse them.

I also recommend creating and editing all your playlists in the cloud, even if you choose to also download them to your device. If you edit a playlist in the cloud, you can always download the updated playlist to your device again, whereas you can't upload a playlist you created or modified on your Kindle Fire back to the cloud.

Deleting a Playlist

When you no longer want to keep a playlist, you can delete it. Deleting a playlist doesn't affect the songs themselves; it only removes the playlist.

When you delete a cloud playlist, it becomes inaccessible to all devices that access your Cloud Player.

1. From the Playlists screen, tap and hold the playlist you want to delete.

2. If you're deleting a cloud playlist, Tap Delete from Cloud. If you're deleting a device playlist, tap Remove Playlist from Device.

3. Tap Yes to confirm the deletion.

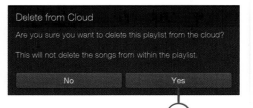

>>>Go Further

ACQUIRING MUSIC FROM OTHER SOURCES

Many other sources for digital music exist, including the iTunes Store and eMusic.com. Music must be in non-DRM AAC, MP3, MIDI, OGG, or WAV format to be accessible on the Kindle Fire. Use the Amazon Cloud Player website to add music to your Cloud Player, or sideload music from Windows Explorer (on the PC) or using the Android File Transfer app (on the Mac). You find instructions for using the Cloud Player and sideloading in Chapter 2.

Watch Amazon Prime videos for free

Watch your favorite movies and TV shows

Create a Watchlist for later viewing

In this chapter, you learn how to take advantage of the video capabilities of your Kindle Fire and explore how you can use your device to watch your own videos. Topics include the following:

→ Navigating the Video Store
→ Working with your video library
→ Using Second Screen

Watching Video on Your Kindle Fire

Your Kindle Fire is an excellent device for watching videos. The Kindle Fire HDX provides high-definition (1080p) video and Dolby Digital sound for a great theatrical experience that you can hold in your hands. Amazon offers more than 100,000 movies and TV shows that you can watch immediately on your Kindle Fire, and if you're a Prime member, you can find thousands of movies and TV shows that you can watch at no extra charge.

Navigating the Video Store

You can rent or purchase movies and TV shows from the Video Store. Amazon automatically synchronizes your playback location so you can start watching on one device and finish on another.

If you're an Amazon Prime member, you can instantly watch many movies or TV shows as part of your annual membership fee. Most of these videos are streamed, so you can watch them only if you have an Internet connection. Some of them, however, are available for downloading to your device for offline viewing.

You can also rent or purchase videos, which gives you the option of streaming or downloading the video to your Kindle Fire for offline viewing at your convenience. Keep in mind that even if a video is offered for free streaming with Amazon Prime, you still pay the rental or purchase fee if you prefer to download it to your device.

Browsing the Video Store

Access the Video Store from your home screen.

1. Tap Videos to access the Video Store.

2. Tap the Search icon to search for videos.

3. Scroll to view recommended titles.

4. Tap See More to view all Prime Instant Videos.

5. Scroll to see videos in other categories.

6. Tap the navigation menu icon or swipe from the left edge of the screen toward the center of the screen to open the Go To menu.

7. Tap one of the Prime Instant Video options to view videos you can watch for free with your Amazon Prime account.

8. Tap a TV Shows option to view television shows you can purchase.

9. Tap one of the Movies options to view movies for purchase or rental.

10. If you've already purchased or rented videos, tap Library to view your video library.

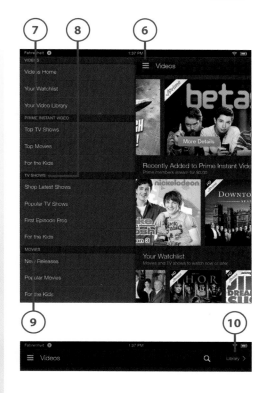

Viewing Movie Details

The Movie Details screen provides viewing options, production information, and the duration of the movie. You might also find a plot overview and reviews of the film.

1. Tap a movie title in the Video Store.

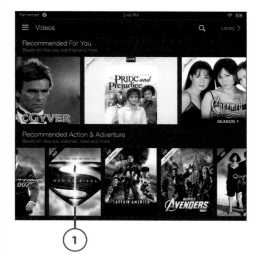

2. Tap Watch Trailer to see the movie trailer.

3. View the rating of the film and the average and total number of reviews the movie has received.

4. View information about the director, release year, and duration of the film.

5. View the viewing period and rental terms if you choose to rent the movie.

6. Scroll down to see cast and other information from IMDb, the Internet Movie Database, and read customer reviews of the movie.

Renting or Purchasing a Movie

You can rent or purchase a movie on your Kindle Fire. A rental enables you to view the movie for a short period of time for a lower price. Purchasing a movie is more expensive, but you can watch the movie whenever you want without time restrictions, the same as when you purchase a movie at a retail store.

1. From the movie details screen, tap the price to rent or purchase the movie.

2. Tap the green Rent or Purchase button to complete your transaction.

3. Tap the Watch Now button to stream your purchase immediately.

4. Tap Download to download the movie to your device for viewing when you are not connected to the Internet.

It's Not All Good

Rented Movies Might Expire Sooner Than You Think

When you rent a movie, it typically expires 24 or 48 hours after you start watching it. However, if you select Watch Now or initiate a download of the video to your Kindle Fire, that also starts the clock on the expiration period. Therefore, if you download a video to your Kindle Fire, pay careful attention to the expiration of the rental.

After you pay the rental fee, you typically have 30 days in which to initiate streaming or downloading the movie before the rental expires, even if you have not yet watched the film. When you initiate a download, Amazon displays a notification informing you that you are about to start the rental period and telling you how many hours you have to watch the movie.

Purchasing TV Show Episodes

Amazon carries hundreds of television shows, from sitcoms to miniseries. Unlike movies, TV shows are not available as rentals.

1. Tap a TV show in the Video Store.

2. Tap to see available seasons and episodes.

3. Tap an episode to see details on that episode.

4. Tap the network name to see more TV shows from that network.

5. Scroll down to see additional information about the series and cast from IMDb and read reviews from other Amazon customers who have watched the show.

6. Tap the episode you want to purchase.

7. Tap Buy HD [Price] to purchase the episode.

8. Tap the green Buy HD button to complete your purchase.

Not Everything Is in HD

Some TV shows, such as early seasons of *Doctor Who,* are available in only one format. If a TV show is for sale in multiple formats, the purchase options reflect those choices.

You may also opt to purchase TV shows in standard definition (SD) to save money, because this format is usually at least $1.00 less expensive due to its lower quality.

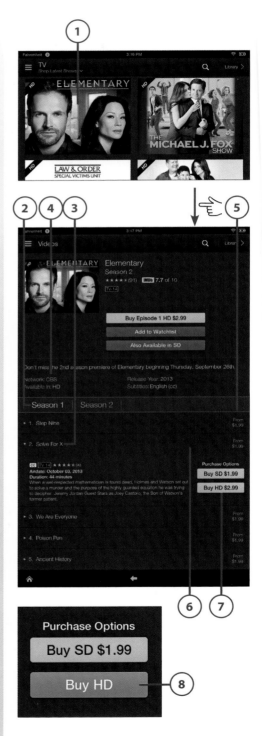

Purchasing Complete TV Show Seasons

If you're catching up on previous seasons or want to complete your collection of a TV series, you can save a little money by purchasing the entire season at once rather than purchasing each episode separately.

1. Tap a TV show from the Video Store.

2. Tap the season you want to purchase.

3. Tap the price to purchase the season.

4. Tap the green Buy button to complete your purchase.

It's Not All Good

Streaming TV Show Versus Purchasing Physical Discs

While streaming or downloading a TV show is fast and easy, it is often the least cost-effective way to acquire episodes or seasons of your favorite programs. Unlike music and books, which are generally less expensive in digital format, purchasing TV shows digitally is usually more expensive than purchasing a physical copy of the show on disc.

Accessing Movies and TV Shows from Prime Instant Video

You can stream movies and TV shows for free from Prime Instant Video. Some, but not all, videos on Prime Instant Video can also be downloaded to your device to be viewed without an Internet connection.

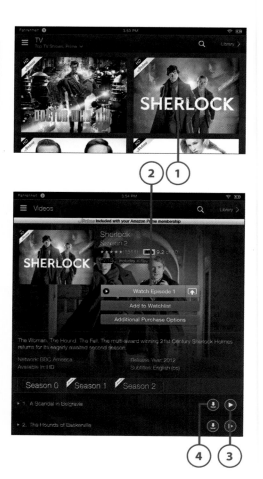

1. Tap a movie or TV show from the Prime Instant Video listing.

2. Tap Watch Episode 1 to begin streaming the first episode of the current season immediately over an Internet connection.

3. Tap the Play button to begin streaming a specific episode immediately over an Internet connection.

4. Tap the Download button to download the episode to your Kindle Fire so you can view it without an Internet connection.

5. In the case of movies, tap Watch Now to begin streaming the movie immediately over an Internet connection.

6. Tap Download to download the movie to your library so you can view it without an Internet connection. If a Prime Instant Video movie is not available for offline viewing, this button does not appear.

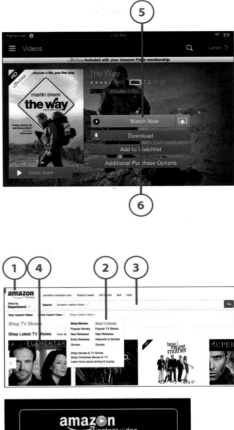

Buying a Season TV Pass

Amazon offers a "TV Pass" for some series. When you purchase a TV Pass, you immediately get the current season's episodes that have already aired, and new episodes of the season are made available to you after they air, often the next day. Although you can view episodes on your Kindle Fire, TV Pass purchases must be made on the Amazon website through a browser.

1. In your web browser, go to www.amazon.com/Instant-Video to access the Video Store.

2. Click (or tap) Shop Instant Video and then Shop TV Shows to browse all the available options.

3. Search for a particular series.

4. Click a current season of a series.

5. Click Buy TV Pass.

6. Click Yes, Continue with My Purchase.

Locating Your TV Pass Videos

Previously aired episodes of a series are immediately added to your Videos library. New episodes automatically appear in your Videos library as they become available.

You can cancel a TV Pass at any time. If you decide to cancel a series, go to Your Video Library on the Amazon site. Click Passes and Preorders, and then click Cancel TV Pass.

Working with Your Video Library

Your video library contains video items that you own, as well as video rentals from the Video Store. Items that you own are always available in your video library unless you permanently delete them. Items that you rent appear in your video library only during the rental period, after which time they disappear.

Your Video Library

You can delete videos from your video library by visiting the Your Video Library page at www.amazon.com/gp/video/library. Simply click a video and then click the Delete link.

Watching a Movie or TV Show

You can stream movies and TV episodes from the cloud to your Kindle Fire as long as you have an Internet connection. You can also watch videos that you've downloaded to your device.

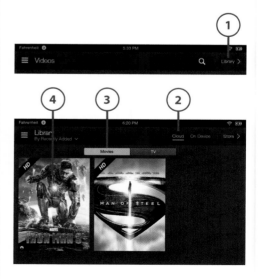

1. From the Videos screen, tap Library.

2. Tap Cloud to see videos in the cloud, or tap On Device to see videos you've downloaded to your Kindle Fire.

3. Tap Movies or TV to locate the video you want to watch.

4. Tap a video you want to watch.

5. Tap Watch Now to watch the video. You must remain connected to the Internet while watching if you're streaming from the cloud.

6. If the video is a rental, a warning appears, notifying you that the rental period is beginning. Tap Start Rental to proceed.

7. While a video is playing, tap the middle of the screen to display the controls.

8. Tap Play/Pause to pause or resume the video.

9. Drag the slider to move to a specific point in the video.

10. Tap the Skip Back button to move backward 10 seconds.

11. Tap the X-Ray info to get more details about an actor in a scene.

12. Tap the Closed Captioning icon and then tap On to display captions for the movie.

13. Tap the Full-Screen button to enlarge the video if it's letterboxed. Tap the button again to return to the original view.

14. Tap the Volume icon and then drag the volume slider to adjust the volume. You can also use the physical volume buttons on the back of your Kindle Fire.

15. Tap the Second Screen button to stream the video to an enabled device, such as a Sony PlayStation 3, to view it on your television.

16. Tap Back to return to the details screen for the video.

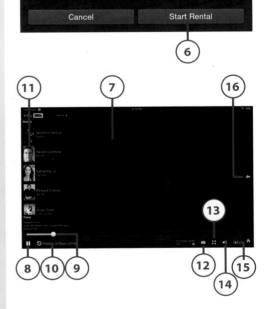

Kindle Lending Library Versus Amazon Instant Video

Unlike the Kindle Lending Library for books, which can be utilized only directly from a Kindle device (not from a Kindle app), you can access Amazon Instant Video from your computer or other devices if you have an Amazon Prime account.

Using X-Ray for Video

Have you ever watched a movie and noticed a familiar actor, but you can't remember where you've seen him? X-Ray for Video tells you which actors are in each scene of a movie. If you want to learn more about an actor, you can get that person's complete film biography from IMDb, the Internet Movie Database. X-Ray for Video also displays trivia about certain videos.

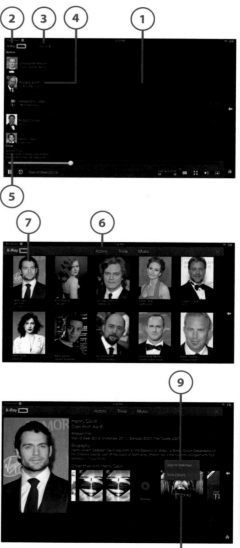

1. While watching a movie, tap the middle of the screen to bring up the video controls.

2. View the X-Ray for Video information on the screen.

3. Tap View All to open the IMDb app and learn more about the movie or TV show in general.

4. Tap an actor's name to get more information about that actor.

5. Tap a trivia item to see the full entry.

6. Tap Actors to view the cast of the video.

7. Tap an actor to get more information about that actor.

8. Tap and hold a film you want to remember to view in the future.

9. Tap Add to Watchlist.

10. Tap Trivia to see a complete list of trivia entries about the video.

11. Tap Jump to Scene to return to the video in the location that relates to the trivia item.

12. Tap Music to see a list of music in the film.

13. Tap Jump to Scene to return to the video in the location that features that song.

14. Tap Buy Soundtrack to purchase the soundtrack from the Amazon Music Store.

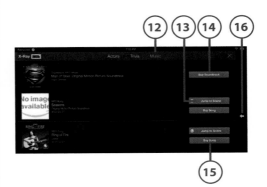

15. Tap Buy Song to purchase the song from the Amazon Music Store.

16. Tap Back to return to your video.

X-Ray for Video Isn't Always Available

Not all videos have X-Ray capabilities. Movies that offer this feature are labeled as such in the Instant Video Store.

Adding a Video to Your Watchlist

As you browse the Video Store, you're likely to find more movies and TV shows than you can possibly watch in one sitting. Instead of purchasing them all at once, add them to your Watchlist so you remember them later.

1. From the Video Store, tap a movie or TV show that interests you.

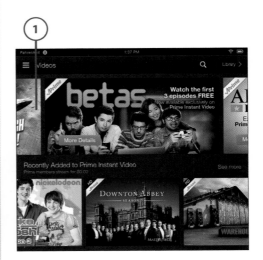

2. Tap Add to Watchlist.

3. Tap the navigation menu button or swipe from the left edge of the screen to the center of the screen to open the Go To menu.

4. Tap Your Watchlist.

Your Watchlist in the Video Store

Your Watchlist also appears on the main screen of the Video Store.

5. Tap Movies to view the movies in your Watchlist.

6. Tap TV to view the TV shows in your Watchlist.

7. Tap a movie or TV show on your Watchlist to open the details screen.

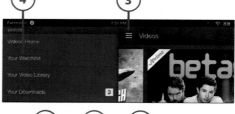

Removing a Video from Your Watchlist

You can remove a video from your Watchlist by tapping the movie or TV show and then tapping the Remove from Watchlist button.

Removing a Downloaded Video

After you've watched a downloaded video, you might want to remove it from your device so that it doesn't take up space. If you own the video, you can download it again at any time.

1. From your Videos library, tap On Device.

2. Tap and hold the video you want to delete from your device.

3. Tap Delete Download.

③

Sharknado

Watch Now

Delete Download

Add to Watchlist

View Movie Details

Cancel

Managing Your Storage Space

Keep in mind that the average HD-quality movie is about 2GB, and the Kindle Fire HDX comes with 16GB up to 64GB of storage. By contrast, Amazon provides unlimited cloud storage for your Amazon purchases. It's best to store the majority of your movies in the cloud and download what you need only when you need it.

Using Second Screen

Second Screen allows you to watch movies and TV shows from Amazon Instant Video on another device, such as your television, while continuing to use your Kindle Fire as a remote control.

To use Second Screen, you must have a compatible device. Right now, the following devices support Second Screen:

- PlayStation 3

- Samsung TVs manufactured in 2013 or later

- Kindle Fire HDX

- Kindle Fire HD 2nd Generation

Although this is a very limited list, more devices should be adding this capability in the future.

Watching Video with Second Screen

To use Second Screen, you must open the Amazon Instant Video app on your Sony PlayStation 3 or Samsung TV.

1. In Videos, tap the movie or TV show you want to watch.

2. On the detail page, tap the Second Screen icon, at the right edge of the Watch Now button.

3. Select the device on which you want to play the movie. If you have not opened the Amazon Instant Video app on the device, the word (offline) appears next to the available device name. In that case, check to be sure you have opened the app.

4. Use the playback controls on your Kindle Fire to control playback of the movie and access X-Ray for Video features.

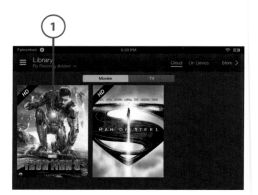

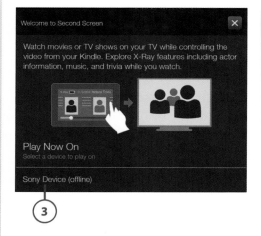

Turn your
Kindle Fire into
a game machine

Enhance the
capabilities of
your Kindle Fire

Connect with your
friends using social
media apps

In this chapter, you learn how to find and install apps from Amazon's Appstore for Android, as well as how to manage and use those apps. Topics include the following:

→ The Appstore
→ Your Apps library
→ Application Settings
→ Games for your Kindle Fire

Installing and Using Apps

You already know that your Kindle Fire is great for reading books, listening to music, and watching video. What you might not realize is that the Kindle Fire is capable of running apps that do a whole lot more. Your Kindle Fire comes with several apps already installed, and it provides access to Amazon's Appstore for Android so that you can get others. Apps that are available from the Appstore on your Kindle Fire device have been tested for compatibility with the Kindle Fire.

The Appstore for Android contains a wide assortment of apps for cooking, education, health and fitness, reference, productivity, shopping, sports, and games. Some of these apps are free; some are not. Unfortunately, you can't return an app for a refund after you buy it, so it's a good idea to read the reviews and look at the screenshots to decide whether an app is a good fit for you before you purchase it.

The Appstore

You purchase new apps for your Kindle Fire in the Appstore. When you browse the store from your Kindle Fire, all the apps listed are compatible with your device.

Appstore for Android from a Web Browser

You can also access the Appstore for Android on the Amazon website (www.amazon.com) on your computer using a web browser, but not all the apps you see listed are compatible with your Kindle Fire. When you view an app from the Appstore for Android on a web browser, look for a check mark for the Kindle Fire, which indicates that the app is compatible.

Compatible devices

Check compatibility

It's Not All Good

Limited Access to Apps

Unlike other Android devices, the Kindle Fire does not provide access to the Google Play Store for Android apps. Amazon touts that its Appstore for Android screens apps for quality, reliability, and lack of viruses. The downside is that its offerings are very limited compared to the Google Play Store, particularly for the types of productivity apps that would make the Kindle Fire a more fully functional tablet.

Browsing Apps

The Appstore offers several tools to make shopping for apps easier.

1. From the home screen, tap Apps to enter the Appstore.

2. Amazon offers a paid app for free every day. Tap to install the free app of the day.

3. Scroll to view additional apps within a category.

4. Scroll to view additional app categories.

5. Tap See More to view more apps within a particular category.

6. Tap the menu icon or swipe from the left edge of the screen to the center to open the navigation menu.

7. Choose an app listing or tap Browse Categories to see all available app categories.

8. Select a category of apps you want to browse.

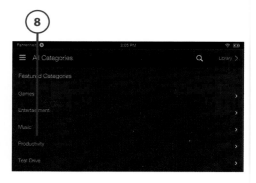

Returning to the Appstore

After you've opened the Apps library for the first time, tapping Apps from the home screen puts you in the Apps library instead of the Appstore. To access the Appstore from the Apps library, tap Store in the top-right corner of the screen.

Viewing and Purchasing Apps

You can view details of an app before you decide to purchase it.

1. Tap an app that interests you.

2. Scroll to view screenshots of the app.

3. Read a description of the app.

4. If the app has a Test Drive mode, tap to try the app before making a purchasing decision.

5. Tap the ratings or scroll down to read reviews from other customers. You can also add your own review of the app.

6. Scroll to the bottom of the screen and read the product details and permissions the app requires. Product details include the file size of the app, so you can control your storage. Permissions might have an impact on your privacy.

7. Tap the price to purchase and install the app. If the app is free, the Price button reads Free.

Testing Driving an App

Most apps force you to make a purchasing decision based on a description, screenshots, and reviews. Some apps, however, offer a Test Drive mode. Test drives are time limited, and all features might not be available, but they generally offer a good idea of what the app has to offer and how well it runs on your Kindle Fire.

1. Tap Test Drive for an app with this preview feature enabled.

2. If this is the first time you've used Test Drive, read the explanation of the limitations on the preview. Tap Continue.

3. Begin using the app. A countdown timer in the top-left corner lets you know how much time you have left for your test drive.

4. Tap the Quit button or the Price button to return to the product description.

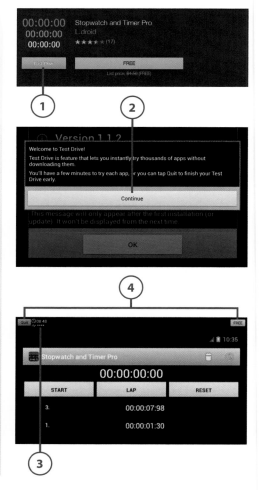

Viewing Subscriptions

Some magazines are available for the Kindle Fire as apps. For example, the magazines *WIRED* and *Time Magazine* both have apps for accessing their content. The apps often offer additional features that aren't available from the Kindle Fire Newsstand. These magazines are typically offered as a free app, but to read the content, you must subscribe on a per-issue or annual basis via the app. You can manage these subscriptions from the Appstore.

1. From the Appstore, tap the navigation menu icon or swipe from the left edge of the screen to the center to open the Go To menu.

2. Tap Manage Subscriptions.

3. Tap a subscription to view details about it.

4. Tap a new subscription period to change subscription details.

5. Subscriptions are set to automatically renew at the end of each subscription period. Deselect Auto-Renew This Subscription to change this behavior.

6. Tap Change Privacy Preferences.

7. Select or deselect the personal information Amazon may share with the magazine or newspaper publisher.

8. Tap Save Changes.

Reactivating Auto-Renewal

After you've turned off auto-renewal, you can turn it back on by tapping Turn On Auto-Renewal in the subscription details.

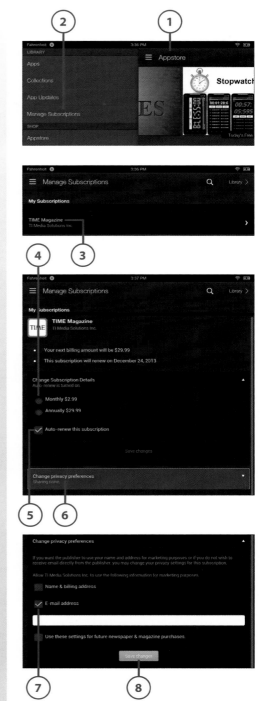

Your Apps Library

Your Apps library contains applications that you have downloaded to your device, as well as applications that you have purchased but not downloaded. When you purchase an app from the Appstore directly on your Kindle Fire, the app is added to your Apps library and installed on your device.

Included Free Apps

Amazon includes some free apps in your Apps library, but not all of them are preinstalled on your Kindle Fire. You'll see them when you tap the Cloud tab in your Apps library.

Browsing Your Apps Library

All your apps are available by browsing your Apps library.

1. From the home screen, tap Apps.

2. Tap Library if the Appstore opens.

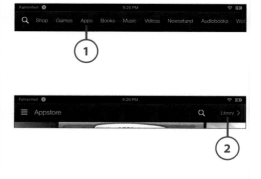

3. Tap Cloud to see all the apps you've purchased, both on your device and in the cloud.

4. Tap On Device to see only the apps that are installed on your device.

5. Tap By Recent to sort your apps according to when they were added to your library.

6. Tap By Title to sort your apps by title.

7. Tap the Search icon to search your Apps library.

Installing a Purchased App

When you purchase an app from the Appstore for Android using your web browser, the app is stored in the cloud. You need to download and install it before you can use it. Installed apps appear in the Cloud listing with a check mark.

1. From the Cloud list in the Apps library, tap the app that you want to install.

2. Wait for your app to download and install. You can tap several apps at a time, and each is queued for download. A check mark appears on the icon when the app is downloaded.

3. Tap an app to open it. After an app has been installed on your device, you can open it from either the Cloud or On Device screen.

Accessing Your Apps

Aside from the Apps library, newly installed apps appear on the Carousel on your home screen.

Adding an App to Favorites

You can add your favorite apps to your home screen for easier access. Find more information on using and organizing your Favorites in Chapter 1, "Getting Started with the Kindle Fire."

1. Tap On Device to see only the apps that you've installed.

2. Tap and hold the app that you want to add to your home screen.

3. Tap Add to Home.

It's Not All Good

Finding Ads in Your Apps

Many free apps are ad supported. You get to use the app for free, but in return, you're presented with ads on the screen. Some apps offer an upgrade to an ad-free version, for a price. If the ads are unobtrusive, you hardly notice them after awhile. In cases where ads interrupt navigation or require you to click to continue, upgrading is well worth the price if you use the app frequently.

Uninstalling an App

Uninstalling an app removes it from your device, but it remains stored in the cloud. You can reinstall the app later without having to pay for it again.

1. Tap On Device to see only the apps you've installed.

2. Tap and hold the app that you want to uninstall.

3. Tap Remove from Device to uninstall the app.

Cannot Uninstall Preinstalled Apps

Contacts, Email, Help, Clock, Camera, Goodreads on Kindle, Kindle FreeTime, Shop Amazon, Silk, and Calendar are all preinstalled apps that you cannot uninstall from your Kindle Fire. Each of these apps serves a purpose on the device.

Updating an Application

Your Kindle Fire automatically updates apps as new versions are released. You can change your update settings to turn off automatic updates or to receive a notice when an app is updated.

1. Swipe down from the status bar to open Quick Settings.

2. Tap Settings.

3. Tap Applications.

4. Tap Appstore.

5. Tap Automatic Updates.

6. Enable Automatic Updates is turned on by default. Deselect this option if you don't want your Kindle Fire to update apps automatically.

7. Tap Notify Me When Updates Are Installed if you want your Kindle Fire to display a notification whenever a new version of an app is installed. Notifications appear in the status bar.

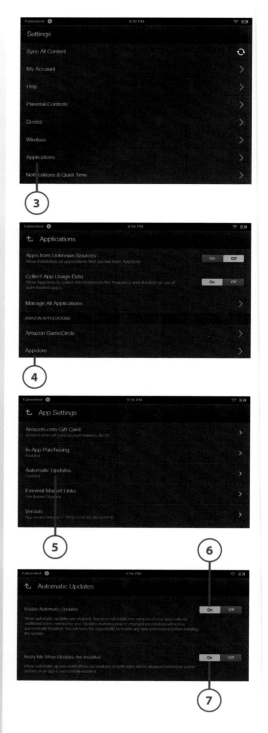

Application Settings

Apps may have bugs that cause them to become unresponsive or crash. This is why apps get updated so often, to fix the problems that become obvious only when a large number of users interact with the app.

In some cases, you might need to force an application to close if it's misbehaving. If an app is behaving unpredictably even after you force-stop it and relaunch it, the app might have some corrupted data in its cache or database. You can force-stop apps and delete app data from the Application Settings screen.

Force-Stopping an Application

If an app is causing problems on your Kindle Fire, or if it hangs and becomes unresponsive, you can force the app to close. This is called *force-stopping* an app.

1. Swipe down from the status bar to open Quick Settings.

2. Tap Settings.

3. Tap Applications.

4. Tap Manage All Applications.

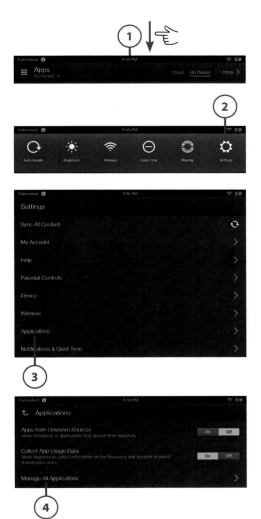

5. Scroll to locate the app you want to stop, and then tap the app that's frozen.

6. Tap Force Stop to stop the app.

7. Tap Force Stop in the confirmation dialog box to force-stop the app.

SHOULD YOU CLOSE YOUR APPS?

>>>Go Further

Even when you return to the home screen or another app or content library, apps remain running in the background. After a while, you might have dozens of apps running on your Kindle Fire.

Unlike some laptop or desktop computer operating systems, the Kindle Fire's operating system is designed to account for many apps running that aren't currently in use. When you switch away from an app, it enters a sleep state in which it doesn't do anything. Some apps are designed to periodically check for content or perform some other task, but they go back to sleep after that task is completed. So, although you can close apps you're not using, it's unnecessary.

Clearing Application Data

If an app is not working properly even after you force-stop it, the app's data might be corrupt. You can clear an app's data in Application settings.

1. While viewing the Manage All Application settings, tap the app whose data you want to clear.

2. Tap Clear Data.

3. Tap Clear Data in the confirmation dialog box.

It's Not All Good

Clearing Data Clears Everything

When you clear data for an app, you clear all settings and any other data that the app has stored, including account and password information. The next time you launch the app, it starts with the default settings. Don't clear data unless you're sure you don't need any information that the app is storing.

Games for Your Kindle Fire

No tablet device is complete without games, and the Kindle Fire is no exception. You can purchase and install games on your Kindle Fire from the Appstore for Android. They appear in the Apps library along with all your other apps.

Games also appear in the Games library. This screen makes it faster to access your games and provides access to certain game-specific features, such as tracking achievements and comparing scores with your friends using GameCircle.

Is GameCircle Necessary?

GameCircle adds a social element to your gameplay, but if that's not your thing, it's easily ignored. Learn more about GameCircle in Chapter 8, "Using Social Media and Chat."

Accessing Games

The Games library contains all apps that the Kindle Fire identifies as games. Developers identify the category of an app when they submit it to the Appstore.

1. From the home screen, tap Games.

2. Tap to download and install the app if it hasn't already been installed, or tap to play the game.

3. Tap Store to enter a special area in the Appstore for games.

4. Scroll to locate a game.

5. Tap Refine and then select a category from the drop-down menu to hone in on the types of games you like to play.

6. Tap a game to view the details page.

7. Tap the Price button to purchase the game. This button reads Free if there is no charge for the app.

8. Tap Get App.

It's Not All Good

Installing Apps from Unknown Sources

Your Kindle Fire provides the capability to sideload third-party apps from sources other than the Appstore. However, I advise against doing so, for a couple reasons. First, many of the apps I tested crashed my Kindle Fire or caused unpredictable behavior. The Kindle Fire version (Fire 3.0) of the Android operating system is highly customized, so features that work well on an Android phone or tablet might not work on the Kindle Fire. Second, Android apps are a common source of Android viruses, and because the Kindle Fire is directly tied to your Amazon account, the risk of installing apps from unknown sources is simply too great to ignore. If you do choose to side-load third-party apps, look for reviews that mention how that app behaves on the Kindle Fire before loading it onto your device.

Make
video calls

Update your
Facebook
status

Talk books
and read
reviews

Check your
Twitter
stream

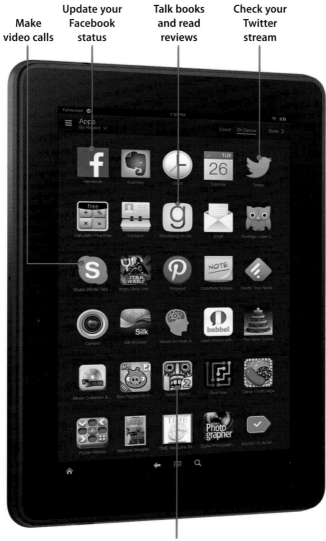

Compare game
scores with
your friends

In this chapter, you learn how to interact with your friends using your Kindle Fire. Topics include the following:

→ Sharing with Facebook and Twitter
→ Talking books with the Goodreads community
→ Video chatting over Skype
→ Sharing game achievements with GameCircle

Using Social Media and Chat

Your Kindle Fire provides several ways for you to connect with friends and family. Share notes, highlights, and final thoughts about the books you read on Goodreads, Facebook, and Twitter. Make free video chat calls using the Skype app and the camera on your Kindle Fire. Compare achievements and high scores in your games with friends on GameCircle.

If you add some free apps to your Kindle Fire, you can also keep up with what your friends are doing on Facebook and Twitter.

Sharing with Social Networks

When you initially set up your Kindle Fire, you are prompted to provide your Facebook, Twitter, and Goodreads logins. Your Kindle Fire makes use of this information in several ways. Whenever you create a note or highlight in a book, you can quickly share it with your Facebook friends and Twitter followers.

It's Not All Good

Social Network Integration Does Not Equal Full Interaction

Adding your Facebook and Twitter information to your Kindle Fire settings enables you to post updates about your Kindle books but does not give you full access to Facebook and Twitter. If you want to post other updates or access your newsfeed, you need to download an appropriate app from the Appstore. These apps are not preinstalled on the Kindle Fire.

Setting Up Your Social Networks

The initial setup sequence for your Kindle Fire asks for your Facebook, Twitter, and Goodreads account information. If you did not provide that information at that time, you can add it later.

1. Swipe down from the status bar to open the Quick Settings.

2. Tap Settings.

3. Tap My Account.

4. Tap Social Network Accounts.

5. Tap the social network with which you want to connect.

6. Enter your account information as prompted, then tap Connect.

7. Follow the prompts to authorize Amazon to link to your account.

8. After linking your accounts to a social network, you can unlink them, if necessary, by tapping Unlink.

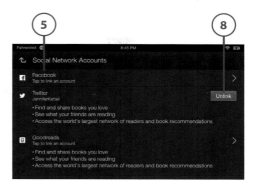

Each Social Media Setup Is Different

The basic steps for setting up Twitter and Goodreads are the same as those above, but the prompts in steps 6 and 7 have slight variations. When entering your account information for Goodreads, for example, tap Sign In rather than Connect. Goodreads also offers the option of using either your Facebook account information or a unique Goodreads account to access the service.

Using the Facebook App

If you want to post status updates or read your newsfeed on Facebook, you need to install a Facebook app. The Appstore offers several apps that can connect to Facebook, including the official Facebook app.

Downloading and Installing the Facebook App

To learn how to locate, download, and install an app from the Appstore for Android, see Chapter 7, "Installing and Using Apps."

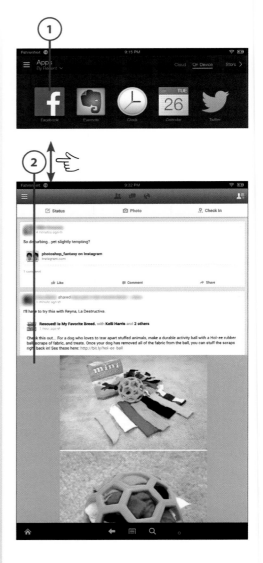

1. Download and install the Facebook app from the Appstore, and then tap the app to open it.

2. The Facebook app automatically uses your account information if you linked your Facebook account to your Kindle Fire. Scroll down to read your newsfeed.

3. Tap the menu button to open the side menu.

4. Tap Messages to view and send private messages.

5. Tap Events to respond to events to which you've been invited.

6. Tap Friends to access a list of all your Facebook friends and any pages you've Liked.

7. Tap a group to access the group's newsfeed.

8. Swipe from right to left to close the menu and return to your newsfeed.

9. Tap the Friends icon to respond to friend requests.

10. Tap the Messages icon to read and send private messages.

11. Tap the Notifications icon to view your notifications.

12. Tap Status to post a status update.

13. Tap Photo to upload a photo from your Photos library.

14. Tap Check In to show your friends your current location.

15. Tap the Chat icon to see a list of who's online.

Some Features Are Not for the Kindle Fire

The Facebook app is designed for all Android devices, including smartphones, so some of the features do not work on the Kindle Fire. Most of the Settings options are designed for Android smartphone notifications, not the Kindle Fire.

Using the Twitter App

Twitter allows you to keep up with your friends in messages of 140 characters or fewer. The Appstore offers several apps that can connect to Twitter, including the official Twitter app.

1. Download and install the Twitter app from the Appstore, and then tap the app to open it.

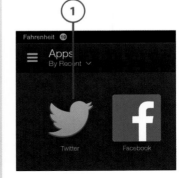

2. Twitter can use your current location to tag your posts so your friends know where you were when you tweeted. Tap OK to allow this or Don't Share if you want to keep your location private.

3. Swipe to read tweets from people you're following.

4. Tap to reply to a tweet.

5. Tap to retweet a message (repost the message so your followers can see it).

6. Tap to indicate that a tweet is one of your favorites.

7. Tap to add new followers.

8. Tap to search for a person or topic on Twitter.

9. Tap to compose a new tweet.

10. Tap to access additional menu options, which allow you to access your account and account settings.

11. Tap to see who has recently followed you and tweets that refer to you.

12. Tap to see trending topics and get suggestions of people to follow.

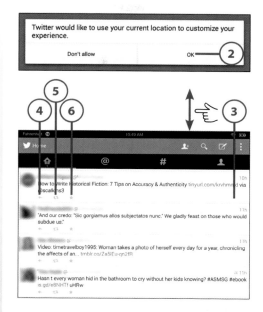

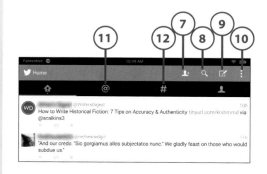

13. Tap to follow someone.

14. Tap to return to your Twitter feed.

15. Tap to view your own account information.

16. Tap to see who is following you.

17. Tap to see who you are following.

18. Tap to edit your Twitter profile or change your settings.

19. Tap to read or send direct messages.

20. View your most recent tweets.

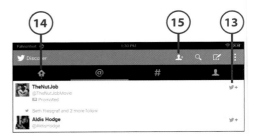

Talking Books with the Goodreads Community

Goodreads is a social network for people who love to read. You can discuss your favorite books and themes, read and post reviews, and meet authors and other readers. Amazon acquired Goodreads in 2012, and the Kindle Fire HDX takes advantage of that relationship by providing several ways for you to connect with the Goodreads community from your device.

Sharing General Comments About Books

As you read a book on your Kindle Fire, you can share your thoughts with the Goodreads community and your friends on Facebook and Twitter.

1. Tap the middle of a page in a book.

2. Tap Share.

3. Enter a comment.

4. Share with Twitter and Facebook, or choose just one of these services. Both services are selected by default if you have linked your Kindle Fire to those accounts.

5. Tap Share.

6. Tap OK to share your comment and return to your book.

Setting Up Goodreads

If you did not configure your Goodreads account in the Social Network settings when you set up your Kindle Fire, you can add it at any time. See the instructions for "Setting Up Your Social Networks" earlier in this chapter.

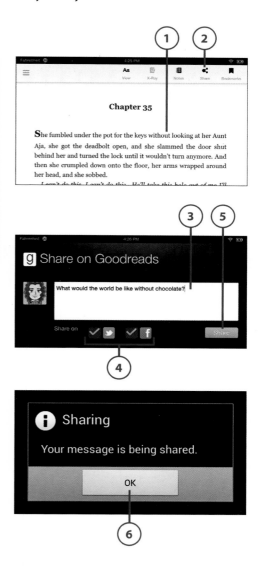

Sharing Highlights from Books

You can highlight key passages in a book to share with your friends on Goodreads, Twitter, and Facebook.

Adding Highlights

Learn how to mark up your books with highlights in the "Working with Notes and Highlights" section of Chapter 4, "Reading on the Kindle Fire."

1. In a book, tap and hold while moving over a passage to select it.

2. Tap Share.

3. Add an optional note.

4. Check to share with Twitter and/or Facebook in addition to your Goodreads friends.

5. Tap Share.

Before You Go in Books

When you reach the end of a book, the Before You Go page appears. Rate and review the book you just read, and share your comments on Goodreads, Facebook, and Twitter.

1. From the Before You Go page, tap Review This Book.

2. Tap the stars to give the book a rating.

3. Type a headline for your review.

4. Enter a review. Your review must be at least 20 words, but it can be quite lengthy, if you prefer.

5. Tap Options.

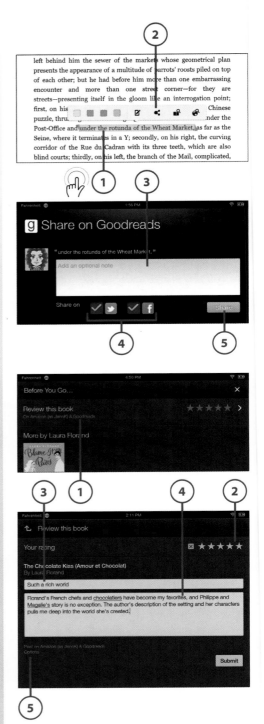

6. Specify if your rating and review should be shared on the Amazon website, on Goodreads, or both.

7. Tap Save.

8. Tap Submit.

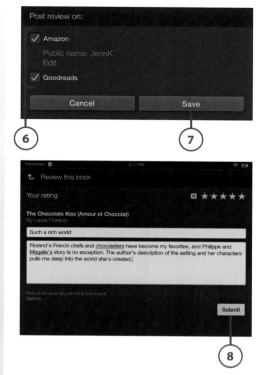

Accessing Goodreads from Your Books Library

Aside from posting comments and reviews to Goodreads from within a book, you can add friends, follow authors, and read updates to your Goodreads feed using the Goodreads for Kindle app.

1. In your Books library, tap the Goodreads icon.

2. If this is your first time using the Goodreads app, tap Continue to set up the app.

3. Tap the book icon to the right of the Want to Read button to add a book you've purchased from Amazon to one of your Goodreads shelves.

4. Tap a shelf to which to add the book.

5. If this is the first time you've added a book to a shelf in the Goodreads app, you'll see a pop-up window explaining the process. Tap OK.

6. When you're finished adding books to your shelves, tap Next.

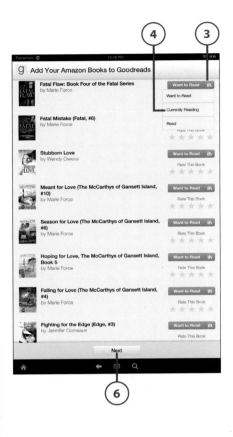

7. Goodreads suggests authors and other readers to follow. Tap Follow to select people from the list.

8. Tap Finish.

9. Scroll to read updates.

10. Tap the menu icon to open the navigational menu.

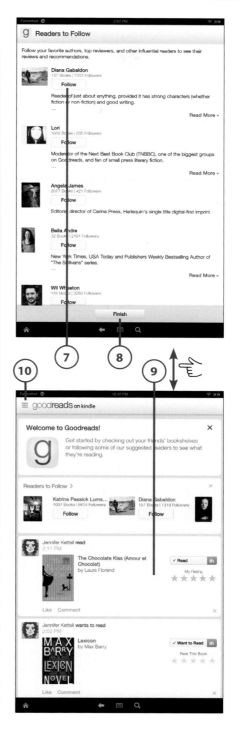

11. Select an item from the menu to view your account, your books, or your friends.

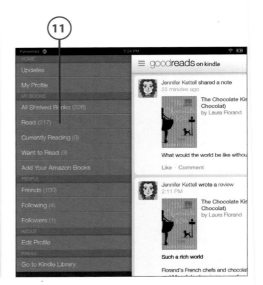

Access the Goodreads App from Your Apps Library

When you tap the Goodreads icon in your Books content library, it opens the Goodreads app. You can also access the Goodreads app from your Apps content library.

Video Chatting Over Skype

Your Kindle Fire has a front-facing camera to facilitate video chat. Skype is a free app that makes video calls to anyone around the world. Put the two together, and you have everything you need to video chat with your friends and family. You can also use it to make free voice calls to other Skype users or buy Skype credits to make regular domestic and international voice calls.

Skype is available for the Kindle Fire, other Android tablets and smartphones, iPhone and iPad, Windows, and Mac. If you want to video chat with someone, chances are, she can install the Skype app to facilitate it.

Setting Up Skype

Amazon adds the Skype account to your cloud account when you register your Kindle Fire, so it's already available for you to download and install.

1. Download and install the Skype app, and then tap the app to open it.

2. Tap Create Account if you are new to Skype, and then follow the prompts to create an account.

3. Tap Sign In with a Skype Account if you already have a Skype account, and then enter your account information.

4. Tap Sign In with a Microsoft Account if you have a Microsoft account (formerly known as Windows Live ID), and then enter your account information.

5. Tap Explore Skype to learn about the Skype app. You can skip this introduction by tapping Skip Tour.

6. Tap the Contacts icon to add Skype contacts.

7. Tap the call icon to dial a number that's not in your contacts.

8. Tap the chat icon to text chat with someone who is not in your contacts.

9. Tap the profile icon to access your account information.

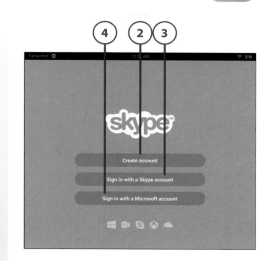

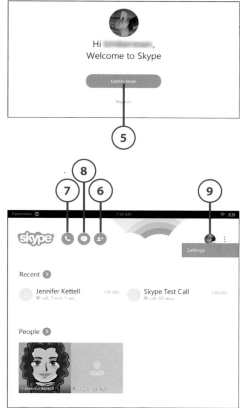

10. Tap Invisible if you don't want other Skype users to know you're online.

11. Tap your photo to change the image that is displayed on your friends' contact lists.

12. Enter a message about your current mood, which is displayed to your Skype contacts.

13. Tap the account credit to learn more about adding funds to your Skype account for placing voice calls to non-Skype users. Add funds on the www.skype.com website, not through the app.

14. Tap View Profile to view your account profile.

15. Tap Sign Out to log out of your account. Use this if you want to log in using a different account.

16. Tap the left side of the screen to close your profile and return to the Skype home page.

17. Tap the More icon to view additional menu options.

18. Tap Settings to access your account settings.

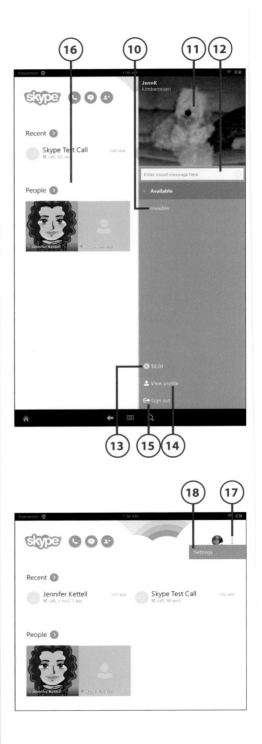

Adding Skype Contacts

Before making a call, add your friends and family to your Skype contacts list.

1. From the Skype home screen, tap the Contacts icon.

2. Tap Add People if you want to search for your new contact by name, or tap Add Number if you want to search by phone number.

3. Enter the name (or phone number) of the person you want to add.

4. Tap the name you want to add.

5. Tap Add to Contacts.

6. Edit the contact request, if you want.

7. Tap Send.

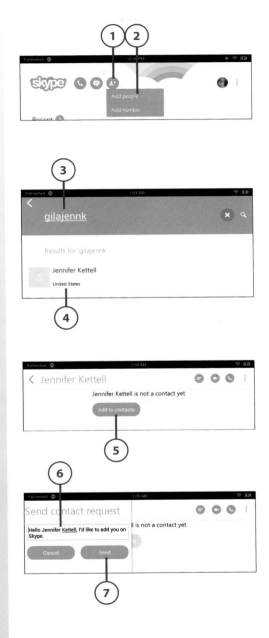

Communicating via Skype

After your contact request has been accepted, the contact is added to the People list on the Skype home screen. You can then initiate a text, voice, or video chat with them.

1. Tap a contact in your People list.

2. Enter text to initiate an instant message (text) conversation.

3. Tap the Video icon to initiate a video chat.

4. Tap the Phone icon to initiate a voice-only chat.

5. Tap the Contacts icon to add another person to a text conversation.

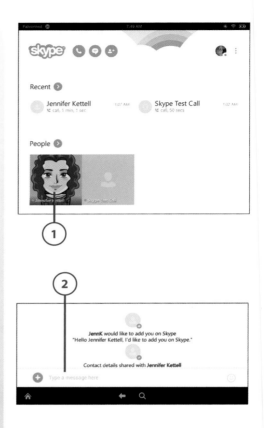

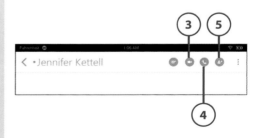

6. When initiating a video chat, your contact's image or avatar appears when the call connects.

7. Tap the Video icon to prevent the person on the call from seeing you. Your image is replaced with your profile avatar.

8. Tap the microphone to mute the sound so that the person on the call can't hear you. Tap it again to restore the sound.

9. Tap the plus (+) icon to add another contact to the conversation.

10. Tap the phone to disconnect the call.

11. To receive a call, tap the green phone button to respond only by voice.

12. Tap the green video camera to respond by voice and video.

13. Tap the red phone to reject the call.

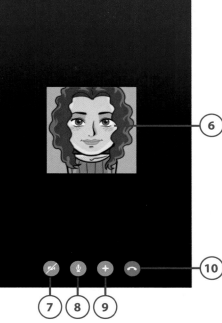

Sharing Game Achievements with GameCircle

Gaming on your Kindle Fire can become a social experience. Although you cannot play a multiplayer game on the Fire and interact with your friends in real-time, you can share your achievements in certain games and challenge your friends to see who can get the highest score.

GameCircle brings this social interaction to your Kindle Fire games. Although you don't have to use GameCircle to play any game on the Kindle Fire, if you want to work to earn trophies or show up your friends, this is a great way to do it.

Identifying GameCircle Games

Not every game can interact with GameCircle. The game developer decides whether to include these features in an app.

1. From the home screen, tap Games. From your Games library, look for a game that shows a series of blue icons to the right of the name. Those are GameCircle-enabled games.

2. Tap to see which achievements you've reached in the game.

3. Tap to see the leaderboard for the game.

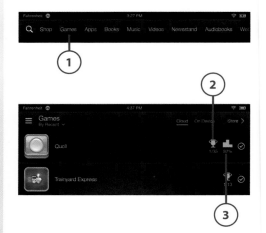

Buying and Installing Apps

If you need help finding and installing apps, see Chapter 7.

It's Not All Good

Finding GameCircle Games

There is no way to quickly distinguish GameCircle games from other games in the Appstore listings. Many games that work with GameCircle don't even mention this in the Appstore description. If you want to find games specifically with the GameCircle feature, open the navigation menu and tap GameCircle Games, and then select games from that list.

Creating a GameCircle Profile

The first time you play a GameCircle-enabled game, your Kindle Fire automatically creates a nonsensical username and profile for you. Fortunately, you can update and customize it to your liking.

1. In the Games library, tap the navigation menu icon or swipe from the left edge of the screen to the center to open the Navigation menu.

2. Tap Profile to see your current GameCircle nickname and avatar.

3. Tap Edit.

4. Swipe to choose a different avatar.

5. Tap to enter a new nickname.

6. Tap Update.

7. Tap the Back button to return to your Games library.

Adding Friends on GameCircle

Share your GameCircle nickname with your friends so they can find your name on the leaderboards.

1. From the Games library, open the Navigation menu.

2. Tap Friends.

3. Tap Add Friends.

4. Enter the GameCircle nickname of a friend.

5. Tap the Search key.

6. When you find the friend you're looking for, tap Friend.

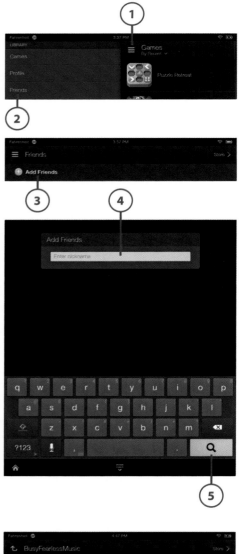

Accessing Game Achievements

Games in GameCircle offer trophies for achievements as you play. An achievement might be to collect a certain number of points or reach a particular level.

1. In the Games library, tap the Trophy icon for a GameCircle game.

2. Scroll through the possible achievements.

3. Track your progress toward an achievement by viewing the completion percentage.

4. Tap Play to play the game.

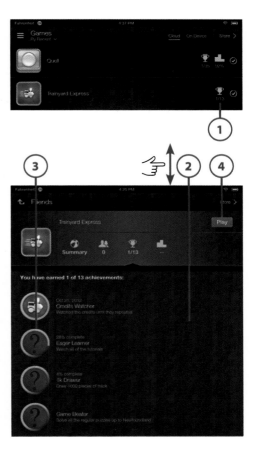

Accessing Leaderboards

The leaderboard shows current high scores for a game. Some games don't have a leaderboard; others have multiple leaderboards for different goals in the game.

1. In the Games library, tap the Leaderboard icon for a GameCircle game.

2. Tap a leaderboard to see the gamers who have reached the top of that chart.

3. Tap Top 100 to see more rankings.

4. Tap a time frame to see top scorers for that period.

5. Tap Play to play the game.

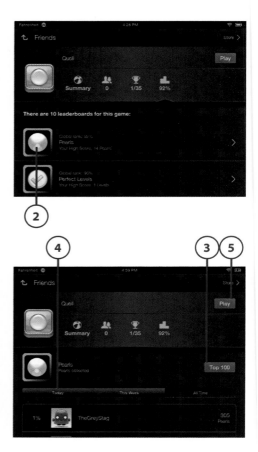

>>>Go Further

FINDING FRIENDS ON THE LEADERBOARDS

If you don't know anyone who plays games on a Kindle Fire, you can find GameCircle friends by checking the leaderboards for the games you play. Tap a nickname, and then tap Friend. The players with the highest scores are the most avid gamers and generally the most willing to make friends in a game.

Combine all your
accounts into one Inbox

Send and receive
attachments

Combined
Inbox   Updated 5:17 PM

Leigh James
Screenshot   5:17PM
Here's the file...

Leigh James
Scrivener questions   5:11PM
Jenn, I'm trying to customize a Scrivener template for a book series. Any ideas on w...

YouTube   Nov 29
Nerdist: "JIM HENSON: The Biography - Panel at New York Comic Con 2013" and...
Check out the latest videos from your channel subscriptions for Nov 29, 2013. Play a...

Quora Weekly Digest   Nov 26
Is there any movie with real computer security cracking (hacking) - Quora
Your Quora Weekly Digest Top content for you this week Is there any movie with real...

YouTube   Nov 22
Geek & Sundry Vlogs: "The Doctor Who Game We Need: Old School Pixel Party with...
Check out the latest videos from your channel subscriptions for Nov 22, 2013. Play a...

Quora Weekly Digest   Nov 19
What's the stupidest thing you've done for love? - Quora
Your Quora Weekly Digest Top content for you this week What's the stupidest thing y...

YouTube   Nov 16
Geek & Sundry Vlogs: "Comics for Whovians: Amy Dallen Talkin' Comics" and more...
Check out the latest videos from your channel subscriptions for Nov 17, 2013. Play a...

Quora Weekly Digest   Nov 12
What are the best stories about people randomly meeting Steve Jobs? - Quora
Your Quora Weekly Digest Top content for you this week What are the best stories ab...

YouTube   Nov 11
Matt Harding just uploaded a video
Matt Harding has uploaded Where the Hell is Matt? Channel Trailer Where the Hell is...

TaraLeigh   Nov 10
Tom...
Whoa http://www.buzzfeed.com/elliehall/15-convincing-reasons-tom-hiddleston-is-...

YouTube   Nov 9

View first two lines
of messages

In this chapter, you learn how to set up email accounts on your Kindle Fire, how to check your email, and how to send email. You also learn how to deal with email attachments. Topics include the following:

→ Email accounts
→ Managing your email Inbox
→ Reading email

Reading and Sending Email

Your Kindle Fire comes with an app for email. You can read your email, send mail, and even view attachments. The Kindle Fire supports various email services, including Gmail, Microsoft mail (Hotmail, Live, Outlook.com), Yahoo!, and POP3 and IMAP servers.

Email Accounts

The first step in using email on your Kindle Fire is setting up your email account. You can set up multiple email accounts on your Kindle Fire. You can then either access each Inbox individually or use the Combined Inbox to see all your messages from all accounts on one screen.

Accessing the Add Account Page

The Kindle Fire makes adding your email accounts easy, whether it's from a service such as Gmail, a Microsoft Exchange account, or a POP3/IMAP account.

1. Swipe down from the status bar to open the Quick Settings.

2. Tap Settings.

3. Tap Applications.

4. Tap Email, Contacts, Calendars.

5. Tap Add Account.

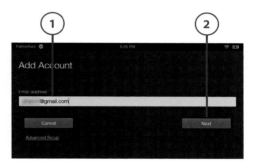

Adding a Gmail, Microsoft, AOL, or Yahoo! Account

If you have an account with a web-mail provider—Gmail, Microsoft, AOL, or Yahoo!—all you need is your email address and password to set up your account on your Kindle Fire.

1. From the Add Account screen, enter the email address for the account you want to add.

2. Tap Next.

3. Enter the password for your email account.

4. Tap Sign In.

5. Review the permissions the email app is requesting of your webmail provider, and then tap Accept.

6. When the setup is complete, tap Go to Inbox to open the email app.

7. Tap Add Another Account to set up additional email accounts.

Using Your Contacts and Calendar

Many services enable you to synchronize the contacts and calendars you have stored on their site with your Kindle Fire's Contacts and Calendar apps. Learn more about these apps in Chapter 10, "Managing Your Personal Documents and Data."

Adding a POP3, IMAP, or Exchange Account

If your email account is through your Internet service provider (ISP) or a private domain, you need to gather more information before setting up your account. Be sure to have your email address, password, IMAP or POP3 (incoming mail) server name, and SMTP (outgoing mail) server name. You also need to know what type of security is used on the mail servers (usually SSL).

1. From the Add Account screen, enter the email address you want to add.

2. Tap Next.

3. Type your password.

4. Tap Next.

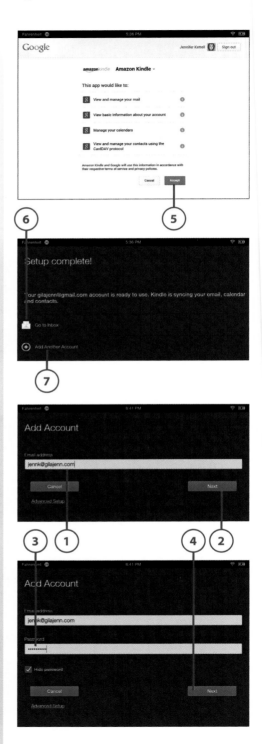

5. Choose an account type—either POP3, IMAP, or Exchange.

6. Enter the incoming server name.

7. Confirm your username. This is usually your email address, but if your host uses a different user-name, enter it here.

8. Confirm your password.

9. Enter your outgoing (SMTP) serv-er. In some cases, this is the same as the IMAP server name.

10. Tap Security Settings and Ports if you need to change the port numbers for the incoming or out-going servers.

11. Tap Next. If any of your settings has an error, you will not be able to move forward until you correct it.

12. When the setup is complete, tap Go to Inbox to open the email app.

13. Tap Add Another Account to set up additional email accounts.

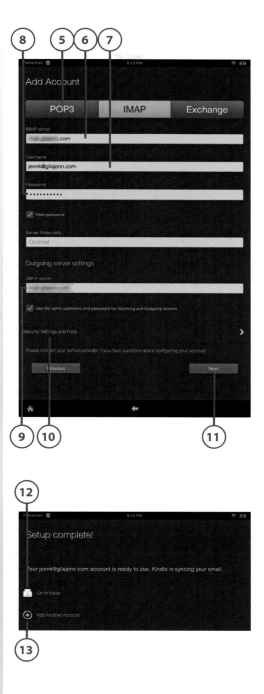

Adding a Microsoft Exchange Account

If you use a Microsoft Exchange account, a type used in many cor-porate settings, you need to know your host server name and your domain name. If you don't know this information, ask your network administrator to help you set up your account.

WHAT'S THE DIFFERENCE BETWEEN IMAP AND POP3?

The POP3 protocol downloads your email onto your Kindle Fire (or your computer or other device). The advantage to this is that your email is available even if you don't have an Internet connection. If you reply to a message, however, it is saved on your device, which means you cannot access it from your other computers and devices. And if your device crashes, your messages are lost. You can optionally configure POP3 to leave messages on the server, but if you read your mail on multiple devices, they are flagged as new on each device. Reading the same messages multiple times is sure to get annoying.

The IMAP protocol connects you directly to the server and keeps your email on the server. This keeps it available to any device you use to access your mail, and all your replies remain available as well. Even if your device crashes, your messages are safe on the server. IMAP also lets you create folders to organize your messages. The only disadvantage to IMAP is that your mail is not available if you cannot connect to the Internet.

If your email provider offers a choice of connecting to your email server through either POP3 or IMAP, I recommend IMAP, especially if you're accessing your messages on multiple devices, such as your Kindle Fire, your computer, and a smartphone.

Modifying Your Account Settings

When you have your email account set up, you can modify the default settings to automatically check mail less frequently or append a text signature to your outgoing messages.

1. Swipe down from the status bar to open Quick Settings.

2. Tap Settings.

3. Tap Applications.

4. Tap Email, Contacts, Calendars.

5. Tap an email account to modify its account settings.

6. Tap the Default Account check box to make this address your default email account when sending email.

7. Turn syncing of email, the calendar, or contacts on or off.

8. Tap to change the frequency with which your Kindle Fire checks for email.

9. Choose a new setting for Inbox Check Frequency.

(7)   **(6)**

Fahrenheit	9:13 PM

gilajenn@gmail.com

Your name
Jennifer Kettell

Description
Gmail

Default account
Send email from this account by default

SYNC AND DATA SETTINGS

Sync Email	On	Off
Sync Calendar	On	Off
Sync Contacts	On	Off

Inbox check frequency
Automatic (push)

Store messages
All

Signature
Append text to messages you send

Reauthorize Gmail account

REMOVE ACCOUNT

Delete account from device   [Remove Account]

(8)

Inbox check frequency

Automatic (push)   ●

Manual   ○

Every 5 minutes   ○

Every 15 minutes   ○

Every 30 minutes   ○

Every hour   ○

[Cancel]

(9)

10. Tap to change how long your Kindle Fire stores old email messages.

11. Select a new duration for storing messages.

12. Tap to create a signature line that's automatically appended to every message you send from this email account.

13. Type a signature line and then tap OK. This is usually your name and title or a message stating that you're typing on your Kindle Fire (which can serve as a warning to recipients that you're not fully responsible for typos).

14. Tap Remove Account to remove this account from your Kindle Fire.

Deleting an Account Deletes Your Data

When you remove an account from your Kindle Fire, all the email, contacts, and calendars associated with that account are deleted. If you remove a POP3 account and did not have your messages saved on the server, those messages are gone forever.

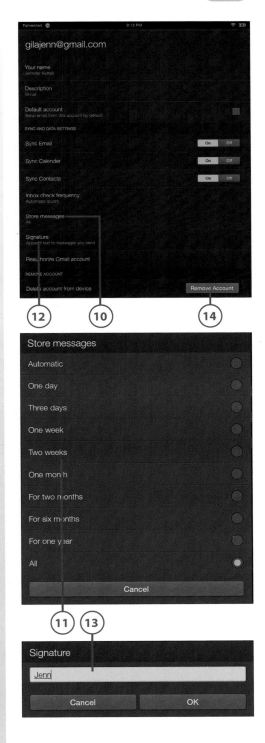

>>>Go Further

CHANGING EMAIL GENERAL SETTINGS

Aside from the settings specific to each account, you can modify the general settings for the Email app. To do this, choose Email General Settings from the Email, Contacts, Calendars page. From the General Settings page, you can change the text size of messages, instruct the Kindle Fire to show or hide images embedded in the messages you receive, and decide whether to quote the original message when you reply to an email.

You can also tell the Kindle Fire to automatically download attachments. I recommend leaving this option set to the default, which is not to automatically download attachments. This protects you against downloading a virus and keeps you in control of how your storage is used on your Kindle Fire. You can always manually download the attachments you want to keep on your device.

Managing Your Email Inbox

The Email app is preinstalled in the Apps library on your Kindle Fire. It is also automatically added to the Favorites on your home screen. When you open it the first time, the app also appears on your home screen Carousel.

Your Inbox is where you can view all the email messages you have received. Without opening a mail message, you can see who sent the mail, the subject of the email, and a brief snippet of the message. You can also flag your mail, sort it, and delete messages you aren't interested in.

Choosing an Inbox

Your Inbox can display email messages from a single account or in a combined account view that shows all messages from all accounts.

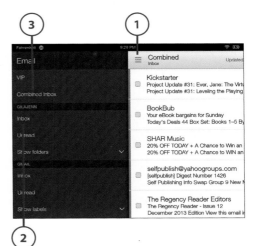

1. From your Inbox, tap the menu icon to open the navigation menu.

2. Tap Inbox under an account name to view the Inbox for that account.

3. Select Combined Inbox to view the Inbox for all the accounts at once.

Determining the Source of a Message

Each email account is color coded when you add it to your Kindle Fire. As you scroll through your combined Inbox, the color of the bar to the left of the message identifies which account it came from.

Choosing a Folder or Label

Most email providers enable you to create folders or labels so that you can organize email that you want to keep. You can choose which folder is displayed when viewing an account's Inbox.

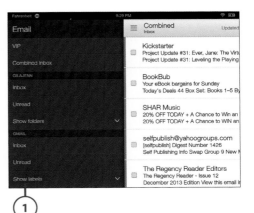

1. From the Navigation menu, tap Show Folders or Show Labels for the account you want to organize.

2. Select a folder or label to display the messages in that folder.

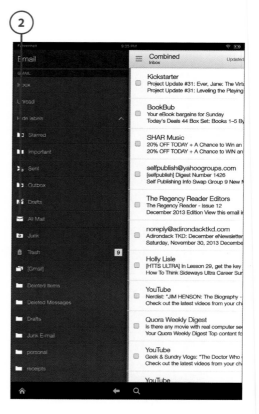

It's Not All Good

Creating Folders

You can use folders on your Kindle Fire, but you can't create them on the device. To create folders for your email account, you have to use an email program on your computer or in your web browser. Those folders are then synced with your Kindle Fire the next time it checks your email.

Searching Email

You can search your email messages.

1. Tap the Search icon.

2. Enter the text you want to search for.

3. Tap the part of the message you want to search.

4. Tap a message from your search results to open the message. You can search the subject, the To field, and the From field for all message types. You can search the entire message for IMAP and POP3 accounts.

5. Tap Cancel to exit the search.

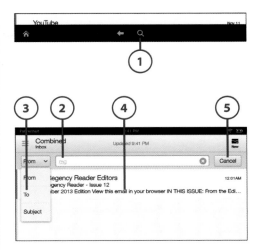

You Can't Search the Text of a Message

The search function in email is very limited. You cannot search the text of a message unless the email account type supports it. IMAP supports full message search, but Gmail does not. If you use the Combined Inbox and one of the accounts doesn't support searching the text of a message, that type of search is unavailable for all messages in the Combined Inbox.

Synchronizing Email and Loading More Messages

Your Kindle Fire automatically checks for mail with the frequency you selected in the account settings. You can manually synchronize at any time to check for new messages between update intervals. The Kindle Fire downloads 25 messages at a time, but you can request more.

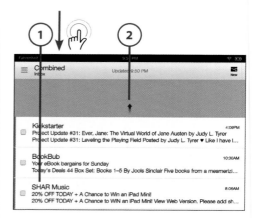

1. From your Inbox, tap your message queue and drag it down the screen.

2. Release the message queue when the arrow at the top of the queue points upward.

3. If there are more messages waiting on the server, a Load More Messages link appears at the bottom of your Inbox. Tap this link to load more messages.

Requesting Additional Messages

The Load More Messages option appears only on POP3 and IMAP accounts. It does not appear when you are in the Combined Inbox.

Selecting and Managing Multiple Messages

You can select one or more messages in your Inbox and then choose to delete them, move them to another folder, or mark them as read or unread.

1. Tap the check box next to the messages you want to select.

2. Tap Delete to delete the messages.

3. Tap Move to move the messages to another folder.

4. Select a folder to move the messages into, and then tap Apply.

5. Tap the More icon to view more options.

6. Tap Flag to mark a message as being important. Flagged messages appear with a gold ribbon to the right of the message heading.

7. Tap Mark to mark selected messages as Read or Unread. This menu item is a toggle, based on whether the selected messages are currently read or unread.

Reading Email

Having email on your Kindle Fire is a great convenience. Not only is it nice to browse your mail while you relax on the couch, but it's also easy to triage your email from the Kindle Fire. By that, I mean that you can quickly peruse your Inbox and delete junk mail or other mail you're not interested in, move mail to another folder, mark important mail for follow-up later, and so forth. Then when you sit down at your computer, you know exactly which messages are worth your attention.

Reading a Message

While reading a message, you can view address details, delete the message, move it to another folder, or flag it.

1. Tap a message in your Inbox to open it.

2. Read the full text of your message.

3. Tap Newer to read the next message in your Inbox.

4. Tap Older to read the next-oldest message in your Inbox.

5. Tap Delete to delete the message.

6. Tap Reply to reply to the message.

7. Tap Reply All to reply to the sender and everyone on the To: or Cc: list.

8. Tap Forward to forward the message and any attachments to a new recipient.

9. Tap the More icon to view more message options.

10. Tap Mark Unread to mark the message as unread in your Inbox.

11. Tap Move to move the message into another folder, and then select a folder.

12. Tap Print to print the message.

13. Tap New Message to compose a new message.

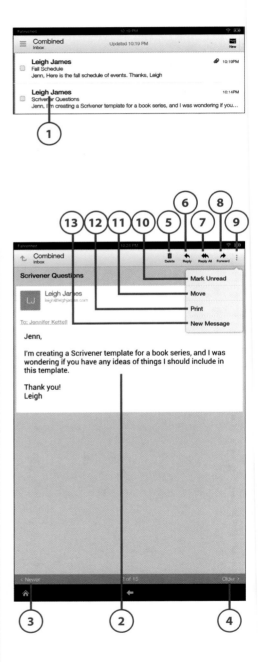

Viewing Attachments

Your Kindle Fire comes with apps that can view many file types, including images, videos in MP4 format, PDF files, and Microsoft Office documents. If you receive attachments in these formats, you can download and access them on your Kindle Fire.

1. Tap a mail message containing an attachment. A paper clip appears on messages with attachments in the Inbox.

2. Tap the attachment. The file downloads, and the icon changes to show the format of the file.

3. After the attachment is downloaded, tap and hold it to open the Attachment menu.

4. Tap Open to open the attachment in an appropriate app.

5. Tap Save to save the attachment onto your Kindle Fire.

Opening Saved Attachments

When you save an attachment, your Kindle Fire automatically puts the file in the appropriate library. PDFs are stored in your Docs library, for example.

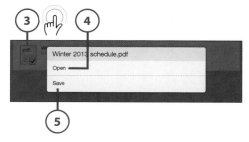

Composing a New Email Message

You can compose a new email either while viewing your Inbox or while viewing a message.

1. Tap the New icon.

2. Enter the email address of the recipient of your message. Separate multiple email addresses with a comma.

3. Tap the plus (+) sign to select a contact from your Contacts app. For more information on the Contacts app, see Chapter 10.

4. Tap the Cc/Bcc link if you want to copy additional people on the message.

5. Enter one or more email addresses in the Cc: field if you want additional people copied on your message.

6. Enter one or more email addresses in the Bcc: field if you want to copy additional people on your message without the other recipients seeing their address(es).

7. Tap your email address in the From: field if you want to change which account sends the message.

8. Enter a subject for your message.

9. Enter the text of the message.

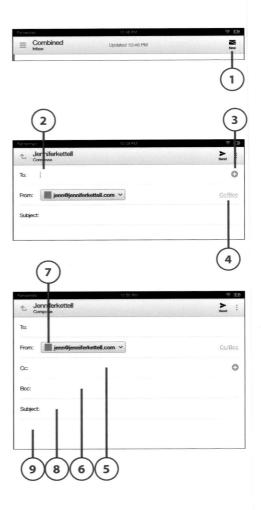

10. Tap the More icon to view more options.

11. Tap Attach (Photo or File) to attach a file to your message.

12. Tap Show Formatting to view formatting options for the message.

13. Tap Save Draft if you want to save the message to edit and send later.

14. Tap Discard Draft to cancel and delete the message.

15. Tap Send to send your message.

Read and edit your personal documents

Manage your contacts

Schedule events

In this chapter, you learn how to maintain the documents and contact information that convert your Kindle Fire from a content viewer into a personal management tool. Topics include the following:

→ Managing Personal Documents
→ Working with Contacts
→ Using the Calendar
→ Archiving old apps and data

Managing Your Personal Documents and Data

Life is messy. You accumulate all manner of bits and pieces of information, phone numbers, and appointments just going about your day. You learned in earlier chapters how to use your Kindle Fire to view content and access apps to connect with friends and manage your email. Until you understand how to use your Kindle Fire to organize those other aspects of your life, though, it won't be a truly indispensable companion.

The Kindle Fire provides tools to organize and retrieve your personal documents, including spreadsheets and Word .doc and .docx files. The Contacts app keeps track of all the people in your life and integrates with the Email app to make reaching them easy.

Managing Personal Documents

In Chapter 2, "Accessing Amazon's Cloud Services," you learned how to use your Cloud Drive and how to sideload to get personal documents onto your Kindle Fire. In Chapter 3, "Using Amazon's Manage

Your Kindle Page," you learned how to email personal documents to your Kindle Fire. No matter which of these techniques you use to transfer documents onto your device, when your documents are in your library, you can easily access them.

Viewing PDF Documents

Your experience in reading personal documents differs depending on what type of file the document is. The Kindle Fire can read PDFs with the built-in Adobe PDF reader.

1. From the home screen, tap Docs.

2. The format of files in your Docs library is evident from the color coding and the format name on the icon. Tap a PDF document.

3. Double-tap to zoom in on the page.

4. Reverse-pinch to enlarge a particular area.

5. Pinch to zoom out.

6. Tap and slide to move around the page.

7. Tap the right side of the page or swipe from right to left to advance one page.

8. Tap the left side of the page or swipe from left to right to go back one page.

9. Tap the middle of the page to display the PDF controls.

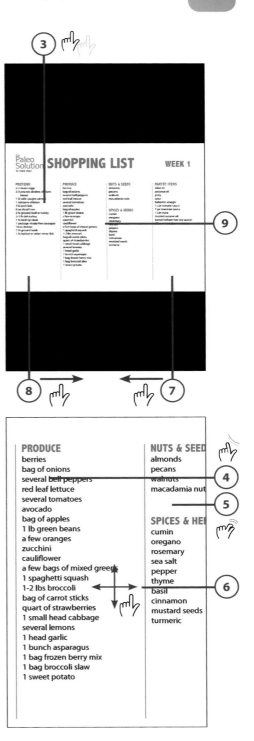

10. Tap a page to jump to that page.

11. Slide the location bar to view other pages in the document.

12. Tap the Back button to return to your Docs library.

Rotating Landscape-Formatted PDFs

PDF documents open full screen, depending on the orientation of your Kindle Fire and the document layout. Rotate your Kindle Fire to landscape orientation for better viewing of landscape-layout documents.

Viewing Word Documents

Personal documents in .txt, .doc, .docx, and .rtf formats open in OfficeSuite. This preinstalled app enables you to view your files and get a word count, but it does not allow you to edit the files.

1. In your Docs library, tap a DOC-formatted file.

2. Reverse pinch to zoom in.

3. Pinch to zoom out.

4. Scroll down to continue reading the document.

5. Tap Find to search the document.

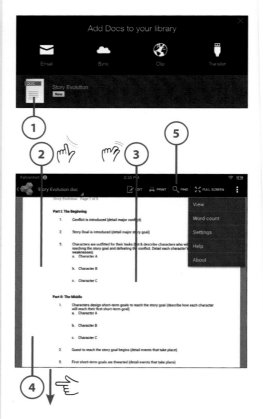

6. Enter your search criteria.

7. Tap Next to see the next occurrence of your search term.

8. Tap Previous to see the previous occurrence of your search term.

9. Tap Done to exit the search.

10. Tap Print to print your document, if you have a Wi-Fi enabled printer.

11. Tap Full Screen if you want to view the document without the menu bars.

12. Tap the More icon to access more options.

13. Tap View to navigate through your document.

14. Tap Go to Top to jump to the top of the document.

15. Tap Go to Bottom to jump to the bottom of the document.

16. Tap Word Count to see how many words, characters, and paragraphs are in the document.

17. Tap OK to return to the document.

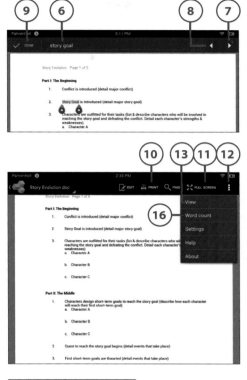

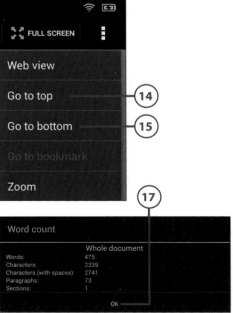

Viewing Spreadsheets

OfficeSuite also enables you to view spreadsheets. Again, you can look at the file and open charts, but you cannot edit the spreadsheet.

1. From the Docs library, tap to open an .xls- or .xlsx-formatted spreadsheet.

2. Double-tap the page to quickly zoom in or out. Use the same gestures to navigate through the spreadsheet as you would a document.

3. Scroll the sheet tabs at the bottom of the screen, and tap a sheet to switch sheets. Not all spreadsheets have multiple worksheets.

4. Tap Sheets to see a list of all the sheets in the worksheet.

5. Choose a sheet.

6. Tap Charts to see any charts that are embedded in the spreadsheet.

7. Tap the menu button to access additional options.

8. Tap Go To in order to find a specific cell.

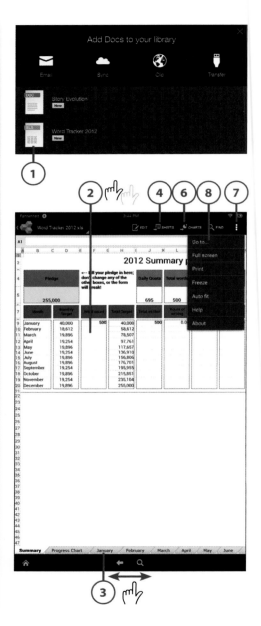

9. Enter the cell coordinates.

10. Tap Go.

Can't Edit Spreadsheets

When you navigate through the cells of a spreadsheet, you can see the formulas that were used to calculate each cell, but you cannot edit them.

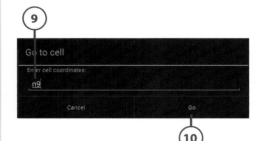

5

Select sheet

Summary

Progress Chart

January

February

March

April

May

June

July

August

September

October

November

December

9

Go to cell

Enter cell coordinates:

n9

Cancel   Go

10

EDITING WORD DOCUMENTS AND SPREADSHEETS

>>>Go Further

If you want to edit documents and spreadsheets on your Kindle Fire, you can purchase one of several Office suites available in the Appstore. OfficeSuite Professional extends the capabilities of the preinstalled OfficeSuite to allow you to edit files. You might want to compare the features in OfficeSuite Professional with those of Kingsoft Office, Documents to Go, or Quickoffice Pro. Each of these apps costs $14.99, but occasionally you can find one listed as the Free App of the Day in the Appstore.

If you plan to edit documents and spreadsheets or do other work that necessitates extensive use of the keyboard, consider purchasing an external Bluetooth keyboard. IVSO and Ionic Pro make Kindle Fire HDX-compatible keyboards with cases for the 7" and 8.9" models.

Using the Contacts App

Your Kindle Fire's Contacts app makes it easy to maintain a list of contacts for email messages or for reference. Your contacts can be synced with your webmail accounts, such as Gmail, and with your Skype contacts.

Viewing Contacts and Marking VIPs

You can view your contacts from the Contacts app. You can also mark your close friends and family as VIPs so you can locate their information faster.

1. Open the Contacts app. You can access it from the Apps library, your Carousel, your Favorites on your home screen, or the Quick Links.

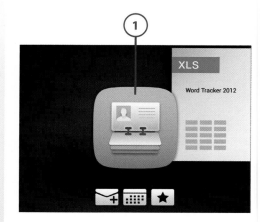

2. Tap and hold the scrollbar to quickly scroll through the alphabet.

3. Tap a contact to view contact details.

4. Tap the star in a contact entry to mark it as a VIP.

5. Tap the arrow to return to the contact list.

6. Tap the menu icon to open the navigation menu.

7. Tap an account to limit the contact list to that account.

8. Tap VIPs to view only contacts marked as VIPs.

VIP Contacts

You can also add a contact to your VIP list by tapping and holding the contact name in your contact list, then selecting Add to VIPs from the pop-up menu.

Adding a Contact

When you meet someone new, add that person's contact information to the Contacts app.

1. Tap the New button.

2. Select which account you want to use to synchronize your contacts. If you did not already set up your accounts in Chapter 9, "Reading and Sending Email," tap Add New Account to link your Kindle Fire with your webmail account.

3. Enter the name information for your contact.

4. Tap the Picture icon to add a picture of the contact. The picture must already be on your Kindle Fire.

5. Enter the phone number.

6. Tap the box to the right of the phone number and select the type of phone number you entered.

7. Enter the email address and select the type.

8. Enter the address and select the type.

9. Tap Add More Fields if you want to enter additional information.

Contacts

You can synchronize your new contact with one of the following accounts. Which account do you want to use?

Amazon
Jennifer Kettell

Gmail
gilajenn@gmail.com

Add New Account

Gmail contact
gilajenn@gmail.com

Name

Add Organization

Phone

Phone | Mobile

Email

Email | Home

Address

Address | Home

Add More Fields

Mobile

Mobile

Work

Home

Main

Work Fax

Home Fax

Pager

Other

Custom

10. Enter your contact's website, birthday, and other information.

11. Tap Save.

Synchronizing Contacts

You can synchronize your contacts with only one account. If you use Gmail or another webmail service to manage your contacts and calendars on your other devices, choose the same account here so that your data stays in sync.

Editing a Contact

You can edit existing contacts.

1. On the contact details screen, tap Edit.

2. Edit information as necessary. Tap the X to delete a field.

3. Tap Save.

Changing Contact Sort Order and Name Display

By default, contacts are sorted by first name, which can make it difficult to easily locate the contact you seek. You can change the sort order of your contacts and how names are displayed.

1. From your contact list, tap the menu icon and then tap Settings.

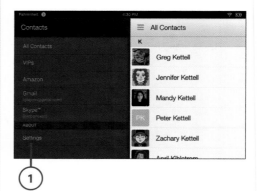

2. Tap Contacts General Settings.

3. Tap Sort Order of Contact Name.

4. Tap Last, First to sort your contacts list by last name.

5. Tap Display Order of Contact Name, and then choose how you want names to be displayed in the contacts list.

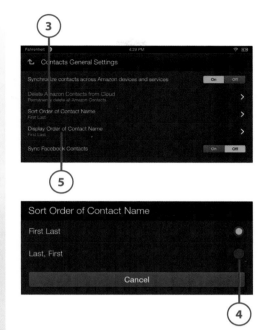

Syncing Contacts from Facebook

While you're in the Contacts General Settings, turn on Sync Facebook Contacts if you want your Facebook friends added to your Contacts app.

Joining Contacts

If you've added multiple email accounts and synced your Contacts app with Facebook, you may see duplicate names in your contacts list. You can combine these duplicates into one entry.

1. Tap and hold a contact that has a duplicate entry.

2. Choose Join.

3. Tap the contact you want to join to the selected contact.

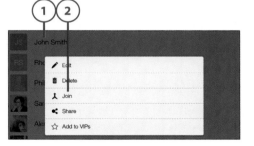

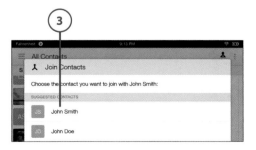

Splitting Joined Contacts

You can split joined contacts back into separate entries. Tap the entry, and then tap Edit. Tap the More icon in the upper right corner of the screen (the vertical dots), and then tap Split. Tap OK when asked to confirm the split.

Deleting Contacts

If you no longer need someone's contact information, you can delete the entry from your Contacts app.

1. Tap and hold an entry in the contacts list.

2. Tap Delete.

3. Tap OK.

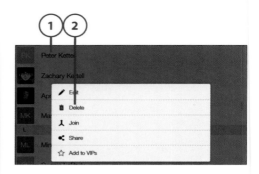

Using the Calendar

The Calendar app on the Kindle Fire helps you keep track of your events and appointments even when you're on the go. You can keep your calendar synced with Google Calendar, Yahoo! Mail, Exchange, Microsoft mail (Hotmail, Live, Outlook.com), and Facebook.

Viewing the Calendar

The Calendar app can be viewed as a daily, weekly, or monthly calendar. You can also opt for a list of events in date order.

1. Open the Calendar app from the Carousel, Apps library, your Favorites on your home screen, or the Quick Links.

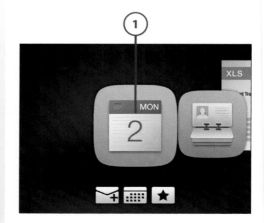

2. Scroll horizontally to view previous or future weeks.

3. Scroll vertically to view additional times of day.

4. Tap Today to return to the current day.

5. Tap an event to see details of that event.

6. Tap the arrow to return to the calendar.

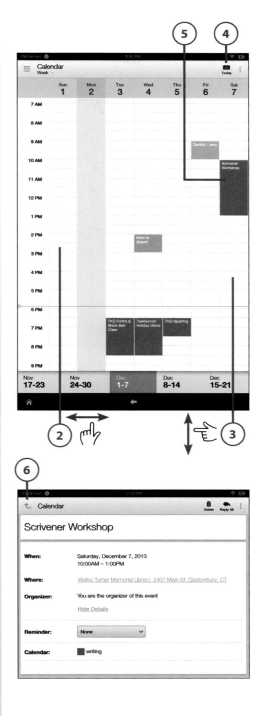

7. Tap Calendar to open the view options, and then tap to select a different view.

8. Tap the menu icon to open the navigational menu.

9. Tap a calendar to remove the check mark and hide it from view on the calendar.

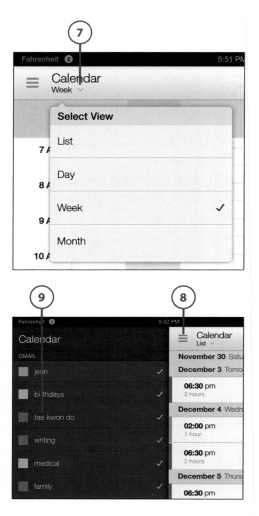

It's Not All Good

Color-Coded Calendars

If you have multiple calendars to keep different members of your family organized or to separate work and home events, you probably rely on color coding to distinguish these events at a glance. Unfortunately, the Kindle Fire Calendar app does not preserve this color coding; instead, it assigns its own colors to each calendar. In many instances, these colors repeat, making it difficult to determine which calendar the event is assigned to unless you tap the event and view the Details.

Adding an Event

When you add events to Google Calendar or another account that is synced to your Kindle Fire Calendar app, it is automatically updated in the app. You can also add events directly to the Calendar app on your Kindle Fire.

1. In the Calendar app, tap the More icon to view additional options.

2. Tap New Event.

3. Enter a title for the event.

4. Enter a location for the event, if you want.

5. Tap the start time.

6. Scroll up or down to set the start time for the event, and then tap OK.

7. Tap the start date.

8. Scroll up or down to set the start date for the event, and then tap OK.

9. Tap to set the end time and date.

10. If this is an all-day event, tap the All Day check box.

11. If the event repeats regularly, tap the Repeat option.

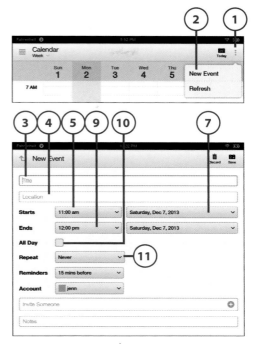

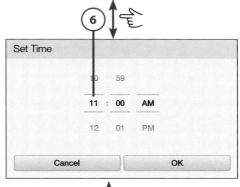

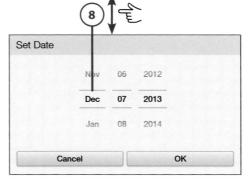

12. Set an interval for the repeating event.

13. If you want a reminder in advance of the event, tap the Reminders option.

14. Set how far in advance you want to be reminded of the upcoming event.

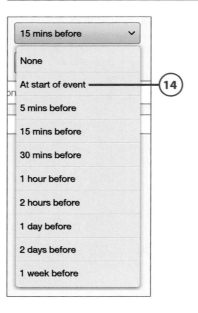

15. Tap Account to change the calendar on which the event appears.

16. Select a calendar for the event.

17. If you want to invite other people to this event, tap Invite Someone and enter their email addresses. You can also press the plus sign (+) to add people from your Contacts app.

18. Tap Notes and enter any other details you want to add about the event.

19. Tap Save to add the event to the assigned calendar.

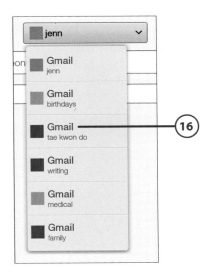

Adding Facebook Events

If you're active on Facebook, you can add your Facebook events to the Calendar app on your Kindle Fire. You can also accept or decline invitations to events from within the Calendar app.

1. Tap the menu icon to open the navigational menu.

2. Tap Settings.

3. Tap Calendar General Settings.

4. Tap the On switch for Sync Facebook Events.

5. Tap Allow.

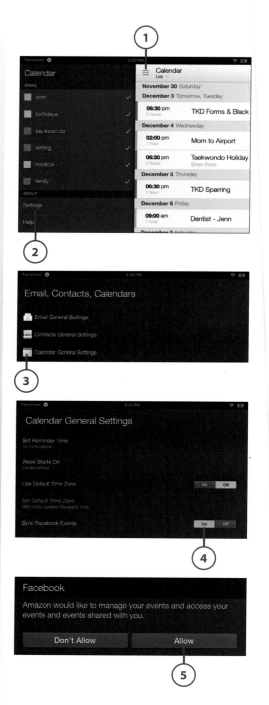

Editing or Deleting an Event

If an event is canceled or your plans change, you can edit or delete the event.

1. Tap an event on your calendar.

2. Tap the More icon to view additional options.

3. Tap Edit.

4. Edit the necessary information for the event.

5. Tap Save to save the updated event.

6. If you want to remove the event, tap Discard to delete the event from your calendar.

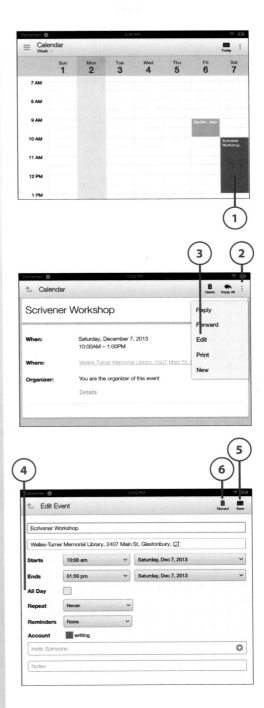

Archiving Old Apps and Data

Unfortunately, storage on your Kindle Fire is not infinite, and you may find your device filling up as you add apps and content. You can easily move content between the Amazon Cloud and your device as explained throughout this book.

Another way to manage your content is to use the 1-Tap Archive. This storage management feature displays items that have not been used in the past 30 days and removes them from your device. You can always download those items back onto your Kindle Fire from the Amazon Cloud at a later date.

Using the 1-Tap Archive

1. Swipe down from the top of the screen to open the Quick Settings.

2. Tap Settings.

3. Tap Device.

4. Tap Storage.

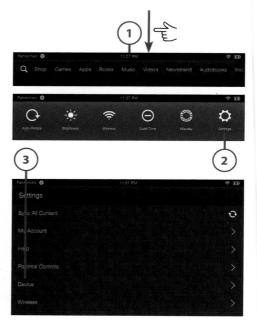

5. Tap 1-Tap Archive.

6. Deselect any items you do not want archived.

7. Tap Archive.

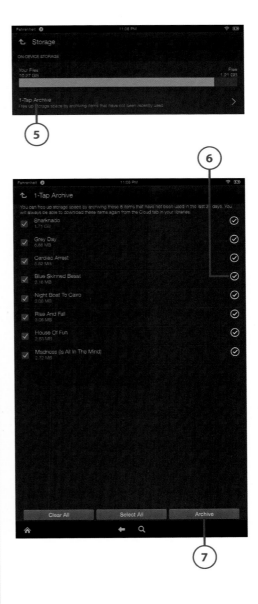

Take pictures with the
dual cameras on your
Kindle Fire HDX 8.9"trends

Take screenshots
of your device
screen

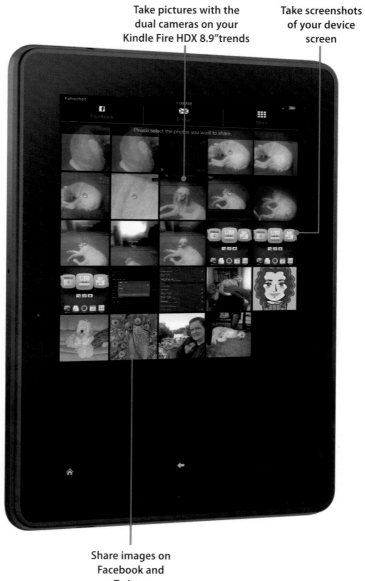

Share images on
Facebook and
Twitter

In this chapter, you learn how to add your personal photos and videos to your Kindle Fire and use the camera features on the Kindle Fire HDX 8.9". Topics include the following:

→ Loading personal photos and videos
→ Using the Photo app
→ Using the cameras on the Kindle Fire HDX 8.9"

Taking Photos with Your Kindle Fire HDX

No tablet device is complete without a camera and the capability to store and manage your photos. The Kindle Fire can even store your personal photos and videos on your Cloud Drive account so your images don't use up the memory on your device.

The Kindle Fire HDX 8.9" comes with two cameras. The front-facing camera offers 720p HD quality, suitable for video calls and selfies. The rear-facing camera is an 8MP (megapixel) with LED flash that offers high-resolution photos and can take 1080p HD video. The Camera app offers many features, including a filmstrip view to see your photos.

The Kindle Fire HDX 7" comes with only the front-facing camera. You can turn your device around to use this camera to take photos, of course, but the features of the Camera app on this device are more limited.

Accessing Personal Photos and Videos

Unless your life is a blank slate, you most likely already have photos and videos that you've taken using other cameras and devices. You can transfer those images to your Kindle Fire.

If you already have photos and videos stored on your computer, you can upload them to your Amazon Cloud Drive, which then makes them available on your Kindle Fire, or you can use the micro-USB cable that came with your Kindle Fire to transfer the photos directly to your device. See Chapter 2, "Accessing Amazon's Cloud Services," to learn how to add files to your Cloud Drive and transfer files via micro-USB cable. You can also upload images and videos from your iPhone or Android phone to your Cloud Drive using the Amazon Cloud Drive apps available from those devices. Images stored in the Pictures folder of your Cloud Drive appear in the Photos library on your Kindle Fire.

Importing Your Facebook Photos

If you linked your Facebook account to your Kindle Fire, as explained in Chapter 8, "Using Social Media and Chat," you can import your Facebook photo gallery into the Photos library. Imported photos are stored in the cloud. You can then download them onto your device, if you want.

1. From the home screen, tap Photos.

2. Tap the menu button or wipe from the left edge of the screen to the center to open the navigational menu.

3. Tap Add Photos.

4. Tap Facebook.

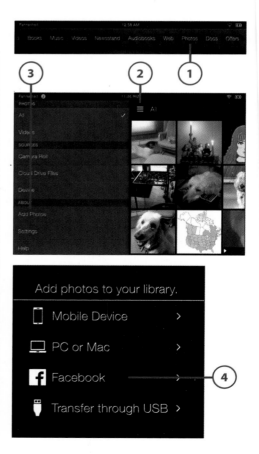

5. Tap Add Facebook Photos.

6. Tap OK to authorize Amazon to import your Facebook photos.

Storing Photos on Your Cloud Drive

Imported Facebook photos are stored on your Cloud Drive. Remember, you have only 5GB of free space on your Cloud Drive. If you're importing a lot of photos, purchase additional cloud storage, if necessary.

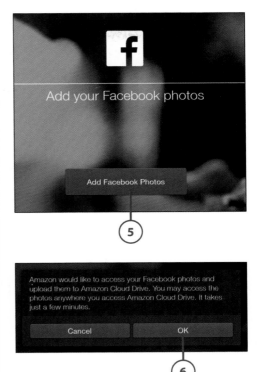

Viewing Photos

After your photos are imported into the Photos library, you can view them full screen on your Kindle Fire.

1. In the Photos library, tap an image.

2. Double-tap an image to zoom in. Double-tap again to zoom back out.

3. Reverse pinch to enlarge the image.

4. Pinch to minimize the image. If you pinch the image to its smallest size, the image closes, and you are returned to the Photos library screen.

5. Tap the image to remove the Navigation and Options bars to view your image without distraction. Tap again to access these navigational aids.

6. Tap the Trash Can icon to delete the image.

7. Tap the More icon to access additional options.

8. Tap Info to view information about the image, such as when the file was created and its full-size dimensions.

9. Tap OK.

10. Tap Download to download the image from the Cloud Drive to your device memory.

It's Not All Good

Missing Accurate Photo Information

The Info window for photos does not provide detailed, accurate information about the photo. Although the dimensions of the image are correct, the Created info tells you only when the image file was copied to your Cloud Drive, not when the image was captured. The Info window also does not provide location or other information that may have been tagged in the original image by your digital camera or mobile device.

Sharing Individual Photos with Other Apps and Social Media

You can share photos with your friends via Facebook, Twitter, and email. You can also share photos with other apps on your Kindle Fire, such as adding a photo to a note in Evernote.

1. When viewing a photo, tap the Share icon.

2. Select an application.

3. Follow the prompts specific to the selected application. If you selected Facebook, for example, you can add a note about the photo, and then tap Post to add it to your newsfeed.

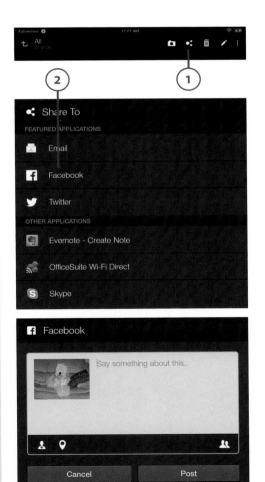

4. If you select Email, enter the email addresses of the people to whom you want to send the photo.

5. Enter the subject of the message.

6. You can add text to the message if you want.

7. Tap Send.

Configure Email before Sharing Photos

If you want to share photos via email, you must first add your account to the Email app. If you have not yet done this, refer to Chapter 9, "Reading and Sending Email," for instructions.

Sharing Photos from the Photos Library Screen

You can also share a photo from the All Photos screen.

1. Tap and hold an image on the All screen of the Photos library.

2. Tap Share.

3. Select an application.

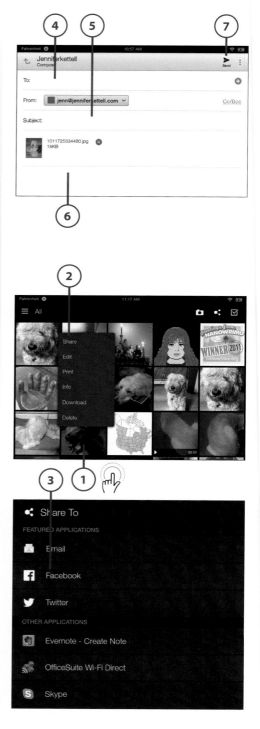

4. Follow the prompts specific to the selected application.

Sharing Multiple Photos

Facebook and the Email app also allow you to share multiple photos at once.

1. Tap the Share icon.

2. Tap the photos you want to share. You must select at least one photo to proceed.

3. Tap Facebook or Email, and then follow the prompts to share photos with those applications.

4. If you want to share multiple photos with other apps, tap More.

5. Select the app with which you want to share your photos, and then follow the prompts specific to that application.

Not All Apps Accept Multiple Photos

You may notice that not all the apps with which you can share an individual photo are available when you attempt to share multiple photos. Twitter, for example, allows you to share only one photo per tweet.

Editing Photos

After you have photos in your Photos library, whether imported from other sources or taken with the Camera app, as explained later in this chapter, you can edit them directly on your Kindle Fire. The editing tools allow you to do everything from adjusting brightness and contrast to adding text and color enhancement effects.

Entering Editing Mode

All the photo editing tools are available from the Edit screen.

1. When viewing a photo, tap the Edit icon.

2. Select an editing tool. You can apply multiple edits to an image.

3. Tap Done to save your changes when you're finished editing the image.

4. Tap the Back button to return to the image without saving any edits.

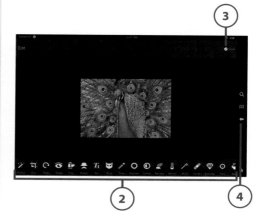

Edit with Abandon

Don't worry about ruining your original images. The Kindle Fire makes a copy of the original image when you enter Edit mode.

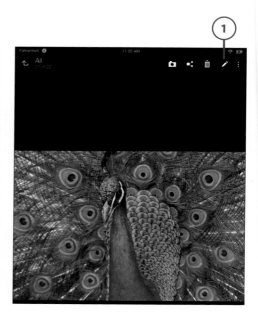

Enhancing a Photo

The Enhance tool makes broad, over-all enhancements to the clarity and lighting of your image.

1. From the Edit bar, tap Enhance.

2. Tap Hi-Def to sharpen the image.

3. Tap Illuminate to enhance the lighting of the image.

4. Tap Color Fix to balance the colors.

5. Tap Apply.

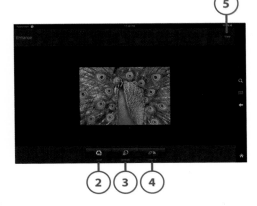

Cropping a Photo

Use the Crop tool to eliminate unwanted parts of the image.

1. From the Edit bar, tap Crop.

2. Select an aspect ratio to adjust the cropping limits to that size.

3. Tap and drag in the center of the crop box to include the area you want to preserve.

4. Tap and drag the corners of the crop box to manually adjust the cropping limits.

5. Tap Apply.

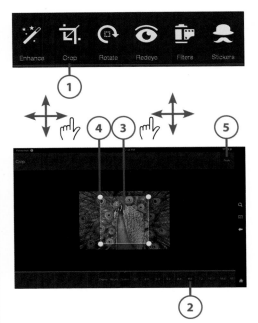

Rotating a Photo

Rotate a photo to adjust an image that's a bit off—or to artfully off-center an image.

1. From the Edit bar, tap Rotate.

2. Tap one of the Rotate buttons to rotate the photo clockwise or counterclockwise. The image rotates 90 degrees every time you tap.

3. Tap one of the Flip buttons to flip the image to its mirror opposite, either horizontally or vertically. If your subject is facing to the left in the original image, flipping it horizontally will result in the subject facing to the right.

4. Tap and drag the white Rotate bar to manually rotate an image. A grid appears over the image to help you align your subject.

5. Tap Apply.

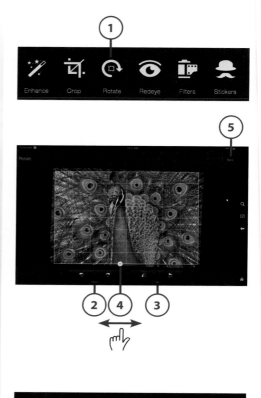

Fixing Redeye

Redeye is caused by a camera's flash reflecting off the back of the retina of your subject.

1. From the Edit bar, tap Redeye.

2. Tap the Zoom icon.

3. Reverse-pinch to zoom in on your subject's eyes, and then tap the Zoom icon to disable zoom mode.

4. Tap a brush size.

5. Drag your finger over the subject's eyes to brush away the redeye.

6. Tap Apply.

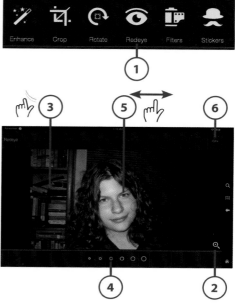

Using the Blemish Tool

The Blemish tool works in the same manner as the Redeye tool. Select the size of the brush and then drag over the image where you want to make the corrections. The Blemish tool feathers the image to hide imperfections.

Using Filters

Filters can change the color scheme of your image, age your photos, and add a vignette appearance. You can even use a filter to turn a full-color image into black-and-white.

1. From Edit mode, tap Filters.

2. Tap a filter to apply a color filter to the image.

3. Tap Apply.

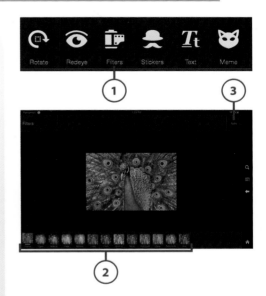

Adding Stickers, Text, or Drawings to a Photo

Stickers, text, and drawings can add a bit of levity to an image.

1. From the Edit bar, tap Stickers.

2. Reverse-pinch to zoom your image, if necessary.

3. Tap and drag a sticker onto the image. You can add multiple stickers.

4. Tap and drag the Rotate icon to rotate or resize the sticker.

5. Tap Apply.

6. Tap Text to add text to the image.

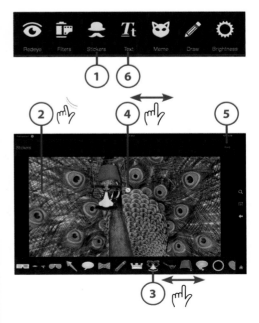

7. Enter text.

8. Tap a color to change the color of the text.

9. Tap and drag the Rotate icon to rotate or resize the text.

10. Tap the center of the text and drag to reposition the text box.

11. Tap Apply.

12. Tap Draw.

13. Tap Zoom.

14. Reverse-pinch to zoom in on your subject.

15. Tap a brush size.

16. Tap a color.

17. Draw on your image.

18. Tap the eraser, and then drag over your drawing if you make a mistake. Only your drawing is erased, not the original image.

19. Tap Apply.

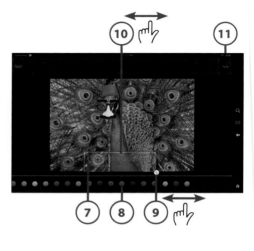

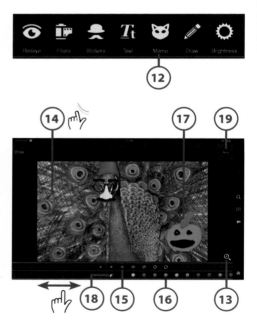

Creating a Meme

The process for adding a meme to an image is similar to adding text. Tap Meme in the Edit bar. Tap the Edit Top Text and/or Edit Bottom Text bars and enter your text. Tap Apply to exit the Meme editor.

The Meme tool is limited to upper case text, and you cannot change the color, size, or rotation of the text. If you want to create a meme-style image without these restrictions, use the Text tool.

Adjusting Brightness, Contrast, Saturation, and Warmth

If your image was photographed under poor lighting conditions, you can make up for those shortcomings by adjusting combinations of settings.

1. From Edit mode, tap either Brightness, Contrast, Saturation, Warmth, or Sharpness.

2. Tap and drag the slider to adjust the image.

3. Tap Apply.

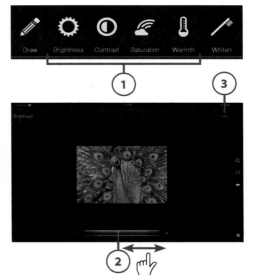

Changing the Focus of an Image

The Focus tool allows you to focus on one area of your image by blurring everything else. (It does not let you bring blurry images into focus.)

1. From Edit mode, tap Focus.

2. Tap a shape.

3. Drag to adjust the shape over the portion of the image that should remain focused.

4. Tap Apply.

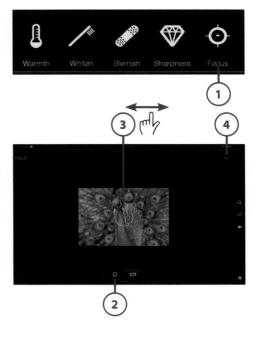

Adding a Splash of Color to an Image

The Splash tool converts an image to black-and-white, and then allows you to add back color only to the areas where you want it to make a splash.

1. From Edit mode, tap Splash.

2. Tap the Zoom icon.

3. Reverse-pinch to zoom in on the image, and then tap the Zoom icon to disable zoom mode.

4. Tap Free Color.

5. Drag your finger over the areas of the image to which you want to add back the original color.

6. Tap Smart Color.

7. Drag your finger over the area of the image where you want to add back a particular original color. The color of the first area you touch is the only color that is restored as you drag your finger across the image. You can lift your finger and tap elsewhere to reset the smart color.

8. Tap Erase, and then drag across the image to undo your changes if you make a mistake.

9. Tap Apply.

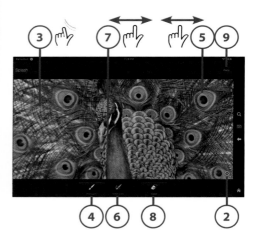

Using the Cameras

The rear-facing camera on the Kindle Fire HDX 8.9" model can be used to take photos or videos. You can then edit your photos using the tools mentioned earlier in this chapter. You can also use the front-facing camera on the Kindle Fire HDX 7" model, but the image quality will not be as good.

Photos and videos taken with the camera are automatically stored in your Cloud Drive. These uploads use up your Cloud Drive storage, so it's important to keep track of your storage and manage it accordingly. If you find yourself running out of storage, refer to Chapter 2 to learn how to purchase additional storage.

Managing Your Photos

An alternative to purchasing additional Cloud Drive storage is to remove the photos you no longer need on your Kindle Fire to your computer, where you can then transfer them to a flash drive or other storage device. To do this, refer to Chapter 2 to learn how to use your micro-USB cable to transfer files to your computer.

Taking Photos

The Camera app allows you to adjust several settings before taking a photo.

1. Tap the Camera app in either the Carousel, the favorites area of the home screen, or the Apps library.

2. Adjust the flash setting. If the Flash icon appears by itself, it is set to On. When the icon has an A next to it, the flash is set to Auto. When it's disabled, the icon appears with an X.

3. If you have a Kindle Fire HDX 8.9" device, tap the Switch Cameras icon to switch between the front- and rear-facing cameras.

4. Tap the Gear icon.

5. To take High Dynamic Range (HDR) images, tap the On switch for HDR.

6. Tap the Camera Roll icon to view the Camera Roll, a subset of the images in your Photos library.

7. Tap the focus area to specify which area of the image should be the focal point.

8. Reverse-pinch to zoom in on an area. You can also use the volume buttons on the back of your Kindle Fire to adjust the zoom.

9. Tap the shutter to take a picture.

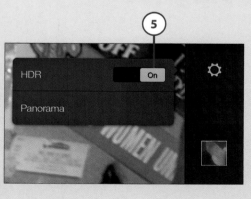

10. Tap the Film Strip icon to view the images you've recently taken without leaving the Camera app.

Accessing the Camera from the Photos Library

You can also access the Camera app from within the Photos library by tapping the Camera icon.

>>>Go Further

UNDERSTANDING HIGH DYNAMIC RANGE

High Dynamic Range (HDR) captures three images whenever you take a picture: an original at normal exposure, one at short exposure, and one at longer exposure. These images are then combined into a single image that enhances both the bright and dark region at once.

By default, the Kindle Fire saves only the combined image. If you want to save the original image along with the HDR image, swipe down from the top of the screen to open the Quick Settings, and then tap Settings, Applications, and Camera. Turn on the Keep Original Image setting.

Taking Panoramic Images

The rear-facing camera on the Kindle Fire can also shoot panoramas, wide-angle images of landscapes or sporting events.

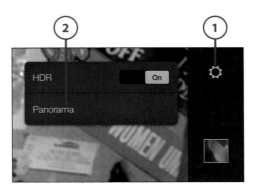

1. In the Camera app, tap the Gear icon.

2. Tap Panorama.

3. Tap the blue button to begin filming your panorama. To cancel, tap the X.

4. Slowly move your Kindle Fire from one end of the area you want to film to the end. You can move horizontally or vertically.

5. Tap the blue button again to stop filming.

6. The Kindle Fire assembles the panoramic image and places it in your camera roll.

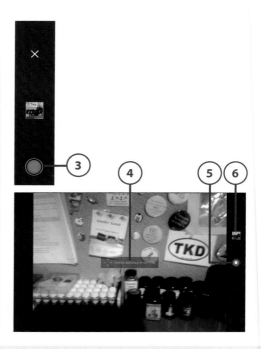

Taking Videos

The Camera app also takes video. You can switch quickly between camera and video modes within the app.

1. Within the Camera app, tap the Camera/Video mode icon.

2. Tap the Record button to begin recording. A counter appears to show the elapsed time of the video. Use the volume buttons on the back of your Kindle Fire to zoom in and out while filming.

3. To capture a still image while filming a video, tap the Shutter icon.

4. Tap the Stop button to end the recording.

Bookmark your favorite sites

See what sites other Kindle Fire users are viewing the most

Browse websites

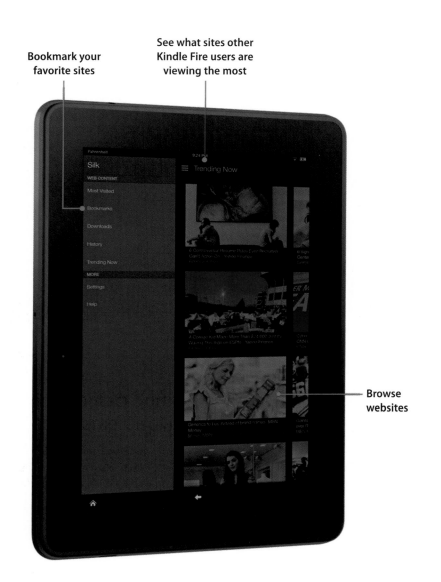

In this chapter, you learn how to use Silk, the web browser that's included with your Kindle Fire. Topics include the following:

→ Browsing the Web
→ Working with tabs
→ Using bookmarks and history

Browsing the Web with Silk

Your Kindle Fire includes a web browser called Silk. Silk is a full-featured browser with support for most of today's modern web standards.

You'll likely find that browsing on a tablet device is a mixed bag. Some sites look and work great; others might not work as well. Tapping a specific link can be difficult when hyperlinks on a page appear too close to each other unless you zoom in on the page. Even with these drawbacks, though, having the capability to browse the Internet from your favorite chair is a great convenience.

Browsing the Web

Silk works similarly to the web browser that you use on your computer. One major difference is that, instead of using a mouse, you use touch to navigate with Silk.

In this section, you learn the basics of using Silk. In the sections that follow, I explain additional features, such as using favorites and tabs, to help you get the most out of Silk.

Browsing to a Website

You can enter a URL and browse directly to a website.

1. On the home screen, tap Web in the Navigation bar.

2. The first time you open Silk, or when Silk opens to a new tab, it displays a list of Most Visited websites. Tap one of those sites if you want to visit it.

3. Tap inside the Address bar and enter a URL. As you type, Silk attempts to home in on the URL you seek.

4. Tap one of the suggested entries when your destination appears. You can also type a complete URL and tap the Go button on the keyboard.

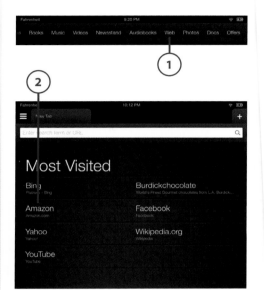

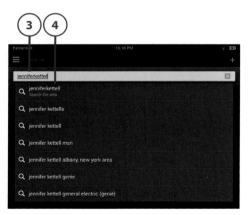

Navigating a Page

Web pages open full screen. You can navigate the page using zoom and pan techniques.

1. Browse to a URL.

2. Double-tap an area to zoom in. Double-tap again to zoom out.

3. Drag to move around the page.

4. Reverse-pinch to zoom in on the page.

5. Pinch to zoom out on the page.

6. Tap a link to follow the link.

7. Tap the Full-Screen icon to remove the Navigation and Options bars and view the page in full screen.

8. Tap the Back icon to return to the previous page.

9. Tap the Forward icon to return to the more recent page.

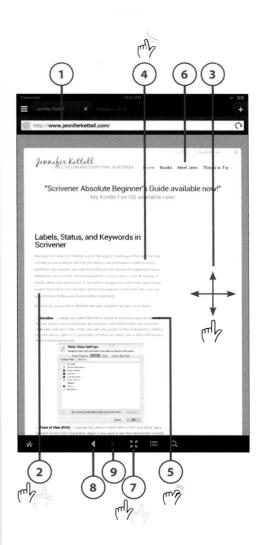

Sharing Pages with Social Networks and Other Apps

When you find a page that you want to share with your Facebook friends, you can do it easily.

1. From the page that you want to share, tap the menu icon in the Options bar.

2. Tap Share Page.

3. Tap the social network or app with which you want to share the page.

4. Follow the prompts for the option you have chosen. If you are sharing the page on Facebook, for example, enter a comment about the page, and then tap Post.

Sharing Pages with Email

You can also share a page by sending a link through email.

1. From the Share To menu, tap Email.

2. Enter one or more email addresses.

3. Add a message, if you want.

4. Tap Send to send from your default email account.

Copying a Link to the Current Page

You can copy a link to the current page so that you can paste it into a document.

1. At the top of the screen, tap and hold the URL in the Address bar.

2. Tap Copy to copy the URL so that you can paste it elsewhere. You can paste the URL on another page within Silk or even in another app.

Pasting URLs

To paste a URL, tap and hold, and then Paste. You can paste into the Address bar in Silk, the subject or text of an email message, or in many other apps.

Copying and Opening Hyperlinks

You can copy a hyperlink to paste it into another app. You can also open that hyperlink in a different tab.

1. Tap and hold a hyperlink.

2. Tap Copy Link URL.

3. If you want to open the link in a different browser tab, tap Open in New Tab.

4. If you want to open the link in a different browser tab without leaving the current page, tap Open in Background Tab.

Saving Images

If you tap and hold an image on a web page, you have the option to save the image in your Photos library.

Searching the Web

Whenever you begin typing in the Address bar, Silk offers the option to search for the term you enter.

1. At the top of the page, enter your search term in the Address bar. The URL that was in the Address bar is replaced with what you type.

2. Tap Go (on the keyboard) or tap a search suggestion to search using your configured search engine.

Your Search Engine

The default search engine is Bing. To change the default search engine to Google or Yahoo!, open the navigational menu and then select Settings. Tap Search Engine and choose from the list.

Working with Tabs

After you tap a link on a website, you can always tap the Back button to return to the previous page, but using tabs is much more convenient. Tabs enable you to have more than one web page open at the same time. You can flip between pages by tapping the tab that contains the page you want to view.

Because each tab is using resources on your Kindle Fire, Silk limits you to a total of 10 open tabs at a time.

Navigating Tabs

You can add a new tab so that you can browse to a new page while leaving the current page open in a different tab. You can then close a single tab or multiple tabs.

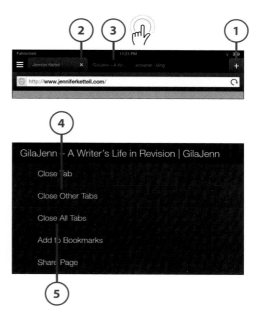

1. Tap the Add Tab icon to add a new tab.

2. Tap the Close icon to close a tab.

3. Tap and hold a tab to close multiple tabs.

4. Tap Close Other Tabs to close all tabs except for the active tab.

5. Tap Close All Tabs to close all the tabs and return to the Most Visited page.

Always One Tab

Even if you tap Close All Tabs, one tab remains open and displays the Most Visited page. If you tap the Close icon on this tab, Silk closes and returns you to the home screen.

Using Bookmarks and History

Bookmarks are an easy way to return to a page at any time. Bookmarks aren't convenient only for saving your favorite sites. You can also use them to temporarily save links to websites while you are researching a particular topic. For example, you can save bookmarks to product reviews so that you can easily refer back to them when deciding which item to purchase.

Bookmarking the Current Page

You can bookmark any page that you are currently viewing.

1. Tap the menu icon on the Options bar.

2. Tap the Add Bookmark button to the left of the Address bar.

3. Edit the name of the bookmark (or you can just go with the default).

4. Tap OK to save the bookmark.

Bookmarking a Hyperlink

You can bookmark a hyperlink without following the link.

1. Tap and hold the hyperlink that you want to bookmark.

2. Tap Bookmark Link.

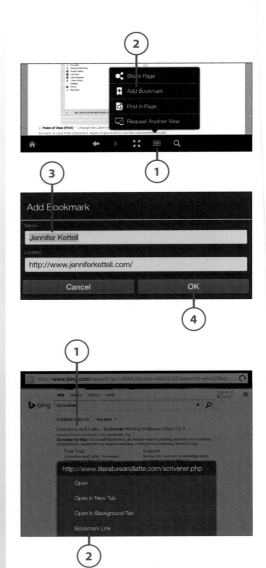

3. Enter a name for the bookmark.

4. Edit the URL, if desired. You can shorten a link to a specific page on a site to the main URL for the site, for example.

5. Tap OK to save your bookmark.

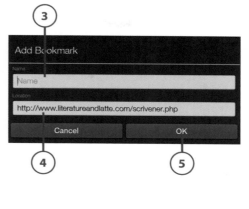

Viewing and Following Bookmarks

You can view all your bookmarks on one page and then tap to follow one.

1. Tap the menu icon or swipe from the left edge of the screen to the center to open the navigational menu.

2. Tap Bookmarks.

3. Tap a bookmark to go to that page.

4. Tap Bookmarks and then select an option to change the sort order.

5. Tap the List View icon to view the bookmarks in a list. Tap the Grid View icon to return to the default view.

6. Tap Add to create a new bookmark without first navigating to the URL.

Editing a Bookmark

You can edit the name or location of a bookmark.

1. From the Bookmarks screen, tap and hold the bookmark you want to edit.

2. Tap Edit Bookmark.

3. Make the desired changes to your bookmark.

4. Tap OK to save the bookmark.

5. Tap Delete to remove the bookmark.

Viewing History

As you browse the Web, Silk keeps a record of where you've been. You can view your browsing history for the past seven days so that you can return to a page you've previously visited.

1. Tap the menu icon or swipe from the left edge of the screen to the center to open the navigational menu.

2. Tap History.

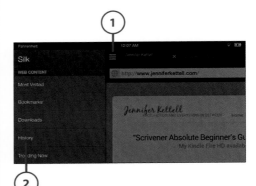

3. Tap a section to expand or collapse the history by that date.

4. Tap an entry to browse to that page.

5. Tap the X to delete that page from your history.

6. Tap Clear All to delete the entire history.

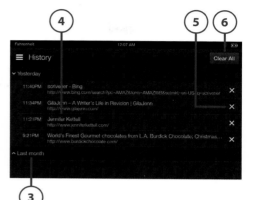

Search is limited
to the child's
content

Each child has a
separate profile
and content

Nonreaders can
locate content by
character or theme

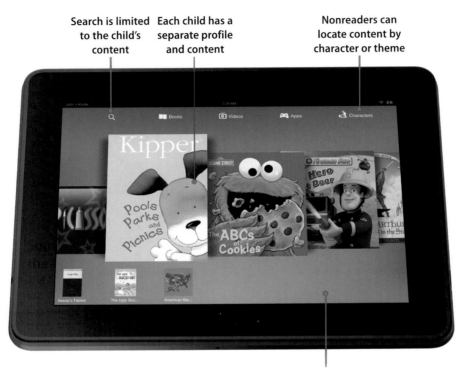

A blue background
lets you see at a
glance that your
child is in FreeTime

In this chapter, you learn how to configure parental controls and Kindle FreeTime to create a safe environment for your child to enjoy the Kindle Fire. Topics include the following:

→ Setting up Kindle FreeTime
→ Teaching your kids how to use Kindle FreeTime
→ Parental controls for older children

Giving Your Kids a Kindle Fire

The Kindle Fire is perfect for kids. The device itself is solid, with a display that's 30 times harder than plastic, so accidental drops and bangs aren't likely to do major damage.

The Kindle Fire offers two types of parental controls. Kindle FreeTime provides a child-friendly, customized interface and allows parents to customize the specific books, music, videos, and apps children can view. The standard parental controls are for older children who are mature enough for the regular Kindle Fire interface and who do not require time restrictions but aren't yet ready to be given free rein over the content they use.

Setting Up Kindle FreeTime

Kindle FreeTime is a preinstalled app that turns your Kindle Fire into a kid-friendly device. FreeTime blocks access to the Silk web browser and the Amazon Store. It disables GameCircle and sharing to the Kindle Community, Facebook, and Twitter. In-app purchases require a password, which prevents your child from making unexpected purchases on your credit card.

You can create a separate profile for each child and give each profile access to specific content. You can set limits on how much screen time each child is allowed on the Kindle Fire. FreeTime also provides a kid-friendly interface for your children, with a blue background and larger font size for text, and a search feature for nonreaders.

FreeTime requires setup before you put the Kindle Fire into your young child's hands.

Accessing Kindle FreeTime

The parent account provides password-protected access to the Kindle FreeTime settings.

1. From the Apps library, tap Kindle FreeTime.

2. The intro screen invites you to subscribe to a free trial of Kindle FreeTime Unlimited. Choose a subscription option or tap No Thanks.

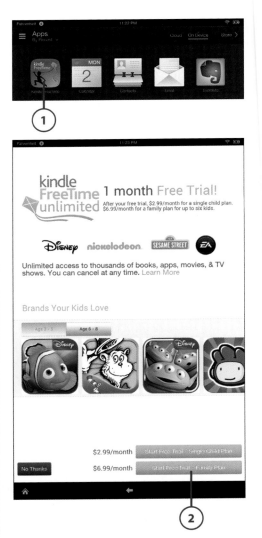

3. Tap Subscribe if you chose to start a free trial of FreeTime Unlimited.

4. Enter your parental controls password. If you have not yet set a password for parental controls, you are prompted to create one.

5. Tap Continue.

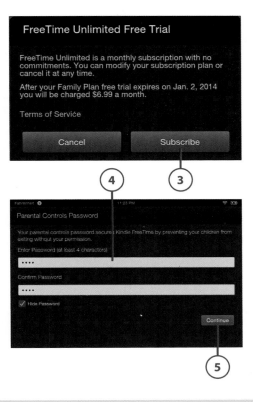

FreeTime Unlimited Free Trial

FreeTime Unlimited is a monthly subscription with no commitments. You can modify your subscription plan or cancel it at any time.

After your Family Plan free trial expires on Jan. 2, 2014 you will be charged $6.99 a month.

Terms of Service

Cancel   Subscribe

Parental Controls Password

Your parental controls password secures Kindle FreeTime by preventing your children from exiting without your permission.

Enter Password (at least 4 characters)

Confirm Password

✓ Hide Password

Continue

>>>Go Further

SUBSCRIBING TO KINDLE FREETIME UNLIMITED

Kindle FreeTime Unlimited is a monthly subscription service that gives your children access to a wide range of age-appropriate books, apps, and videos from Disney, Nickelodeon, Sesame Street, and more. It costs $2.99/month for a single child or $6.99/month for a family subscription (for up to four children) if you have a Prime account. If you do not have a Prime account, the cost is $4.99/month for one child and $9.99/month for a family plan.

If you choose to take advantage of FreeTime Unlimited, consider the maturity and reading level of your child before choosing an age range for their Kindle FreeTime profile. If your preschooler is already reading, the content offered to him/her at the 3–5 year-old account level may not be challenging enough. If this is the case, consider changing the age on your child's account profile.

Setting Up Child Profiles

Each child in your family can have an individual profile on Kindle FreeTime.

1. After you enter your parental controls password, you're immediately prompted to create a child profile. Enter your child's name.

2. Select your child's gender.

3. Tap to enter your child's date of birth.

4. Use the sliders to set your child's birth date, and then tap Done.

5. Tap to set a photo for the profile.

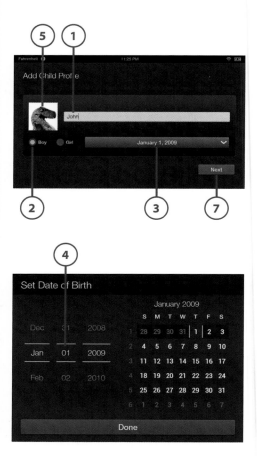

6. Tap an avatar your child can use to identify the profile.

7. Tap Next.

8. Tap Add New Profile to set up additional profiles, and then repeat steps 1–7. You can create up to six profiles on your Kindle Fire.

Completing Profile Setup

After you set up child profiles, the FreeTime app opens to the start page whenever you open the app in the future. If you need to change a profile or add another child, tap Manage Child Profiles on the start page.

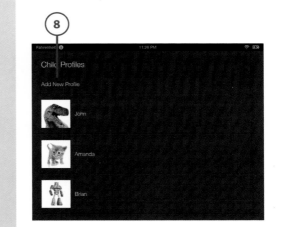

Manage Content on FreeTime

After creating a profile for each child, you can customize the settings so your children each have access to the content you think is appropriate.

Shop First, Add Content Later

Kindle FreeTime does not have access to the Amazon Store, so purchase content for your children before opening FreeTime to manage content for the first time. Of course, you can always add more content to your child's profile when you make future purchases. You must purchase videos for use with FreeTime. You cannot add video rentals or free content from Prime Instant Video to child profiles.

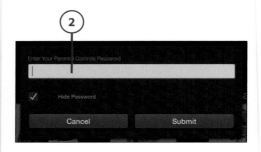

1. From the FreeTime start page, tap Manage Content & Subscription.

2. Enter your parental controls password, and then tap Submit.

3. Tap Add Titles to [Your Child's] Library.

4. Tap the content box to filter the list to a particular type of content.

5. Tap the box to the right of each title you want to add to the profile.

6. Tap Add All Kids' Titles to add all of the titles listed on the screen.

7. Tap Done.

8. Tap the Back button to return to the FreeTime start page.

Unsubscribing from FreeTime Unlimited

If you want to cancel FreeTime Unlimited, tap Unsubscribe from the FreeTime Unlimited option on the Manage Content & Subscription screen.

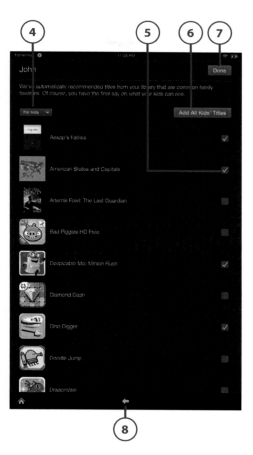

Setting Daily Time Limits

You can set time limits for how long your child can use the Kindle Fire. Alternatively, you can define different limits for each type of content, such as allowing unlimited reading time but only one hour for apps.

1. From the FreeTime start page, tap Daily Time Limits.

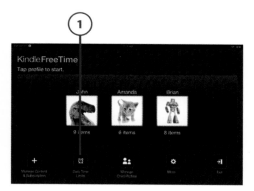

2. Enter your parental controls password, and then tap Submit.

3. Tap a child's profile.

4. Tap On. The screen expands to open the time limit controls.

5. Use the slider to set a total daily usage limit for the Kindle Fire.

6. Tap Time by Activity to set limits based on type of content.

7. Use the slider to set a time limit for Reading Books.

8. Use the slider to set a time limit for Watching Videos. The slider adjusts in 15-minute increments.

9. Use the slider to set a time limit for Using Apps. This setting does not distinguish between educational apps and games.

10. Tap the Back button. From the Time Limits page you can tap the Back button again to return to the start page or another profile to set further time limits.

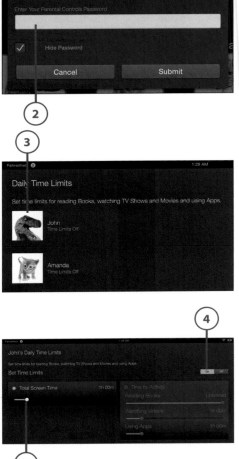

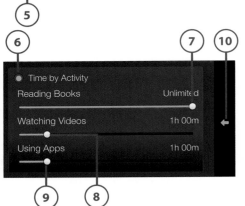

>>>Go Further

SHOULD I SET A LIMIT ON READING BOOKS?

Most parents want to encourage their children to read, so the default setting for reading books on FreeTime is Unlimited. If your child has vision problems, however, you might want to limit overall screen time, to foster time away from the screen. Also, studies have shown that backlit screen time just before bed can affect a child's sleep, so you might want to encourage reading traditional paper books (or E Ink–based devices such as Kindle Paperwhite) at bedtime.

Changing the Parental Controls Password

You can change your parental controls password.

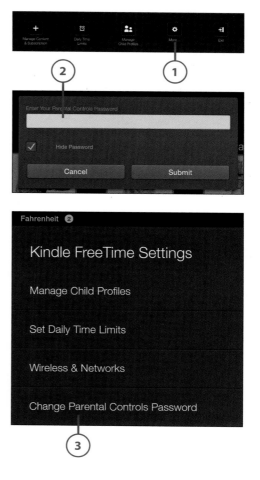

1. From the FreeTime start page, tap More.

2. Enter your current parental controls password, and then tap Submit.

3. Tap Change Parental Controls Password.

4. Enter your current password.

5. Type a new password.

6. Reenter the new password.

7. Tap Finish.

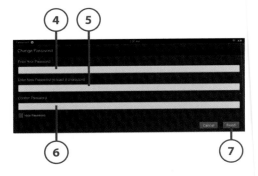

It's Not All Good

Remember Your Password

If you forget your parental controls password, you need to restore your Kindle Fire to factory settings. This wipes out all your Amazon account information, downloaded content, and personal documents, photos, and videos.

If you need to restore your Kindle Fire to factory settings, swipe down from the status bar to open Quick Settings and then tap Settings. Tap Device and then tap Reset to Factory Defaults. Be sure you've first backed up any personal content you want to keep to your Cloud Drive or computer.

Teaching Your Kids How to Use Kindle FreeTime

After setting up FreeTime, tap a child's profile from the start page to enter that child's FreeTime account. The Kindle Fire interface changes to a controlled, kid-friendly environment. The content that you have added to the child's profile is available in the appropriate Books, Videos, and Apps categories. Content also appears on the Carousel.

If you have subscribed to Kindle FreeTime Unlimited, your child will have access to a wide assortment of additional content in addition to what you've added to his or her profile. Books, videos, and apps that are available through Kindle FreeTime Unlimited can be downloaded by your child by tapping on the item from the Carousel or content libraries without any assistance from you. If you purchase additional books, movies, or apps for your child, however, you need to use the Manage Content & Subscription option on the parental controls screen to add them to your child's profile.

It's Not All Good

Controlling Additional Content on FreeTime

Although Amazon screens FreeTime Unlimited content for age-appropriateness, you may have your own ideas of what types of material you want your child to access, particularly content that has product or movie and television tie-ins. If this is an issue for your family, you will want to supervise your child's use of the device, even when the child is within the relative safe zone of FreeTime.

Using the FreeTime Interface

Although children seem to inherently know how to operate electronic devices, and the FreeTime interface is very intuitive, here are some tips for you to help your child get started.

1. From the FreeTime app, tap your child's profile.

2. Swipe along the Carousel to browse new or recently read books, apps, and videos.

3. Tap Books, Videos, or Apps to see what's available.

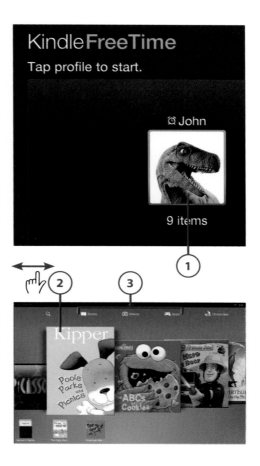

4. Tap a book, video, or app to open it.

5. The Back button takes you back to where you were.

6. The Search button lets you look for a book, app, or video on your account.

7. Tap and hold a book, video, or app to add it to your Favorites on the home screen.

8. Tap Add to Home.

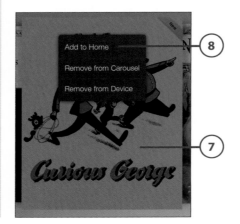

It's Not All Good

Removing Content

Although it seems illogical in such an otherwise controlled environment, your child can remove content from the Kindle Fire by tapping and holding an item and then choosing Remove from Device. If your child inadvertently does this, you must add the content to the profile again for your child to have access to it.

Navigation for Nonreaders

If your child is not yet reading, the Characters option on the Home screen lets your child choose books, videos, and apps based on the characters or theme of the content.

1. From the home screen, tap Characters.

2. Choose a character or theme.

3. Choose a book or app to open.

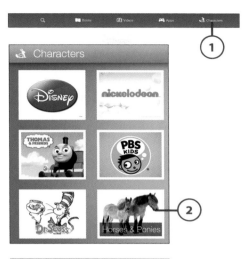

You Can't Choose How Content Is Categorized

The Characters groupings are not perfect. Content is sorted by Amazon, not by the parent, so you cannot control which characters and themes appear or whether a book, video, or app is included or excluded from that grouping.

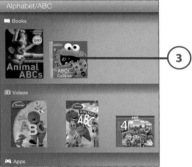

Exiting FreeTime

When it's your turn to use your Kindle Fire, you can exit FreeTime.

1. Swipe down from the status bar to open Quick Settings.

2. Tap Exit FreeTime.

3. Enter your parental controls password, and then tap Submit.

Changing Settings

Your child can access Quick Settings to adjust the brightness of the display. If your child attempts to exit FreeTime or access any other settings or parental controls, the Kindle Fire prompts your child for a password.

Parental Controls for Older Children

If you have slightly older children, they might be ready to use the standard Kindle Fire interface and have more freedom over how much time they spend using the Kindle Fire. As a parent, however, you might still want to limit your child's access to the Internet, email, and other content.

The Kindle Fire's regular parental controls are much less restrictive than those of Kindle FreeTime. In addition to blocking types of content or apps, you can password protect access to the Amazon Store and Instant Video to prevent your child from making unauthorized purchases or downloading inappropriate content.

It's Not All Good

You Cannot Control Content by Rating

You can disable access to an entire content library, such as Videos or Books. However, you cannot control access to content by rating. If your child has access to the Videos library, for example, he or she can watch any video you have purchased on the Kindle Fire. If your child has access to the Books library, he or she can read that copy of *50 Shades of Grey* you purchased for your morning train commute. If you share your Kindle Fire with your children and worry about them accessing your content, consider limiting them to a FreeTime profile.

Setting a Parental Controls Password

Parental controls are password protected.

1. Swipe down from the status bar to open Quick Settings.

2. Tap Settings.

3. Tap Parental Controls.

4. Tap On to turn on parental controls.

5. Enter your parental controls password, and then tap Submit. This is the same password used in the FreeTime app. If you have not yet created a parental controls password, you are prompted to create one.

Managing Parental Controls Settings

After you enter your password, the Parental Controls screen displays several options to limit your child's use of the Kindle Fire.

1. Tap Web Browser to block or unblock access to Silk.

2. Choose which other features should be blocked.

3. Tap the On or Off button for the Password Protect Purchases option. When this is On, purchases from the Amazon Store or the Amazon Shop app require a password. This includes in-app purchases.

4. Tap the On or Off button to password protect video playback. When On, this option requires a password to play Amazon Instant Video and Prime Instant Video.

5. Tap Block and Unblock Content Types to control access to content libraries.

6. Tap the Unblocked button to the right of any content type to toggle the button and block access to that content library.

7. Tap Back to return to the Parental Controls screen.

8. Tap Change Password to change the parental controls password.

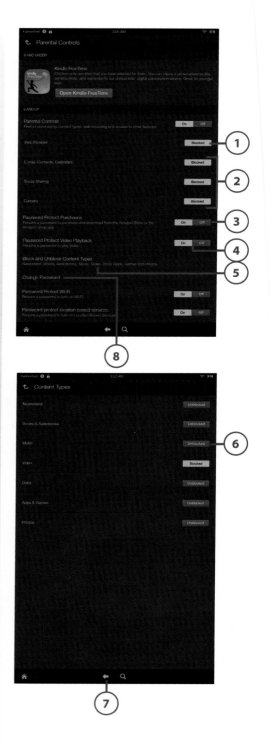

9. Enter your current password.

10. Enter a new password.

11. Reenter the new password to confirm it.

12. Tap Finish.

13. Tap the On or Off button to Password Protect Wi-Fi. When On, this setting requires the parental controls password to turn on Wi-Fi in order to download or stream content.

14. Tap the On or Off button to Password-Protect Location-Based Services. When On, this setting requires the parental controls password to turn on location-based services.

Turning Off Parental Controls

If you want to turn off parental controls, return to the Parental Controls settings screen and tap the Off button.

Index

My **Kindle Fire HDX**

Jennifer Kettell

que

Safari
Books Online

FREE
Online Edition

Your purchase of *My Kindle Fire HDX* includes access to a free online edition for 45 days through the **Safari Books Online** subscription service. Nearly every Que book is available online through **Safari Books Online**, along with thousands of books and videos from publishers such as Addison-Wesley Professional, Cisco Press, Exam Cram, IBM Press, O'Reilly Media, Prentice Hall, Sams, and VMware Press.

Safari Books Online is a digital library providing searchable, on-demand access to thousands of technology, digital media, and professional development books and videos from leading publishers. With one monthly or yearly subscription price, you get unlimited access to learning tools and information on topics including mobile app and software development, tips and tricks on using your favorite gadgets, networking, project management, graphic design, and much more.

Activate your FREE Online Edition at
informit.com/safarifree

STEP 1:   Enter the coupon code: BQPZGAA.

STEP 2:   New Safari users, complete the brief registration form.
Safari subscribers, just log in.

If you have difficulty registering on Safari or accessing the online edition,
please e-mail customer-service@safaribooksonline.com